SUPERTRAINS

Aaron E Klein

Bison Books

Published by
Bison Books Ltd
Kimbolton House
117A Fulham Road
London, SW3 6RL
England

ISBN 0 86124 203 3

Printed in Hong Kong
Reprinted 1989

*Half title: The prototype of French National Railways'
High Speed Train, the TGV, undergoes trials in 1978.*
*Title page: The Empire Builder on the Burlington Route
in 1947.*
*This page: An experimental linear motor car of Japanese
National Railways. This form of propulsion may well
provide an energy-efficient means of transport for the 21st
century.*

CONTENTS

INTRODUCTION

When jet aircraft replaced the likes of DC-3s and rumbling Constellations, and when the sprawl of the superhighway spread from its American birthplace to much of the rest of the world, there were those who predicted the imminent end of passenger railway service. That prophecy came close to realization in the United States, and presented a very real threat and challenge to railways in all of the industrialized world.

Fortunately for those of us who think that a world without railways would be a dull one indeed, there was a sufficient number of far-seeing railway managers who responded to the challenge. They saw that the only way to compete effectively with airlines and automobiles was to provide fast and luxurious service. The result of these efforts are the supertrains.

Just what is a supertrain? I define a super train as one that is incredibly fast, lavishly luxurious or possesses various combinations of these two qualities. Of course, not everyone will agree with my inclusions and some will be annoyed with my exclusions. And there is always the possibility of a train rising to super train contention after this book has been published. The Blue Train of

South Africa, for example, is not at all fast, but it could well be the most luxurious train in the world. Thus it is included here as a super train. Similarly, the Orient Express is outdated by today's standards, but the luxury and legend surrounding this train accord it a special status.

I have approached the problem of differing terminology by using whatever term is in use in the area under discussion. For example, trains run on 'railroads' in the United States and on 'railways' in Europe. The guiding wheels of locomotives and cars are 'trucks' in the United States and 'bogies' in Europe. Hence you will see 'bogie' in the chapter on European super trains and 'truck' in the North America chapter.

The future of train travel is still uncertain. However, many of the trains discussed in this book represent the best hope of trains continuing to run in the next century and beyond.

The five ages of motive power on the Burlington Route range from the classic American steam 4-4-0, through the streamline era to the vastly more powerful diesels of today.

The Origins of Luxury

One day in 1837, a young man got on a Great Western Railway train in London to travel some 20 miles to a young lady's house for the purpose of courting her. A young man courting a pretty girl was not particularly unusual in 1837. However, the young man was Prince Albert of Saxe-Coburg-Gotha, and the house to which he was traveling was Windsor Castle, wherein the newly installed Queen Victoria waited to be courted. That someone of such importance as the future Prince Consort deliberately chose to ride on a railway train was unusual indeed in the 1830s. Public railways had only been in existence some 12 years when Albert went courting. At the time, few railway owners could be accused of overspending on matters of passenger comfort and safety. So, in most places, train travel was not particularly comfortable, and it was not without danger. There were many who thought the Prince extremely irresponsible for taking such chances with his royal person.

The directors of the GWR were, of course, overjoyed, and were quickly filled with heady thoughts of the Queen herself riding on their trains. In anticipation of that event, the GWR, in 1840, fitted out a special car – a royal saloon – at its own expense, and eagerly awaited the Queen's call. However, some two years were to go by before the Queen chose to avail herself of the royal saloon.

The first user of the royal saloon was the dowager Queen Adelaide, in August 1840. King Frederick William IV of Prussia used it in January 1842 on the occasion of his visit to England to attend the christening of the Prince of Wales (the future King Edward VII). Six months after that event, the Queen abruptly informed the railway that she wished to to use the royal saloon for a trip to London. In less than 48 hours, a special train was assembled around the royal saloon and the trip was made without incident.

As it turned out, Queen Victoria liked traveling by train, and she became a frequent rider on many of Europe's railways. Her favor encouraged the building of private railway carriages for much of Europe's royalty. These private carriages were not limited to royalty. Anyone rich enough to pay for it could have one built, and the building of these cars proliferated in the second half of the nineteenth century, in Europe and America.

Private cars, either for royalty or wealthy merchants, were fine showpieces, generating valuable publicity. But everybody knew you couldn't run a profitable railway from just hauling private carriages, and many a railway man of the time would have told you that it wasn't particularly easy to make money from any kind of passenger

A Wagons-Lits parlor car, complete with piano, used on the Trans-Siberian Express in the 1900s.

service. Then, as now, many railways tended to regard passengers as necessary evils. The private carriages did show that it was possible to travel by train in comfort, if not luxury, and they started a trend that resulted in a better deal for the railway passenger in matters of speed, comfort and safety, an idea that eventually led to the idea of the super train.

The entrepreneurs who started the early railways had coal on their minds, not passengers. The first public railway equipped with steam locomotive-hauled rolling stock was the Stockton and Darlington of England, which began service on 25 September 1825 with much fanfare and ceremony. In a bill submitted to Parliament some 25 years earlier, the company asked for powers to build a railway for '. . . the conveyance of coal, iron, lime, corn and other commodities from the interior of the county of Durham to the town of Darlington and the town and port

Stockton.' There was no mention of passengers. Nevertheless, there were some 600 excited passengers riding in carriages of various descriptions on opening day.

Passengers on early railways soon discovered that taking a short joy ride on a bright sunny day was one thing, and traveling longer distances by rail was quite another. While some efforts were made to provide at least a modicum of comfort for passengers paying higher fares, those who traveled at the cheapest fares were barely tolerated. Some railways, particularly in England, carried their lowest fares in open wagons, where they were exposed to smoke, cinders and whatever the

The first supertrain of them all – George Stephenson's immortal Locomotion. This working replica, faithful in every detail, is being prepared for a cavalcade to mark the 150th anniversary of the opening of the Stockton & Darlington Railway in 1825, an event which marked the birth of the Railway Age.

CATCH POINTS

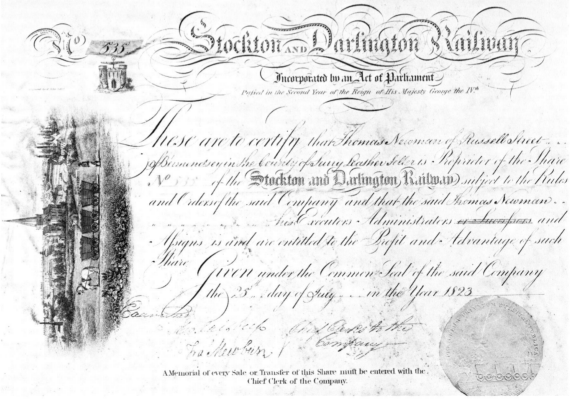

The Stockton & Darlington Railway was opened in 1825. The event marked the beginning of the railway as a public transportation system. Shown here is an original share certificate and Stephenson's Locomotion, which took part in the centenary celebrations of the railway in 1925.

weather had to offer. There were cases of passengers dying of exposure in these cars. Some railways treated cheap fares as if they were freight, allowing them to ride only if there was space for them after freight had been loaded. Often there were no seats, or at best, a plank placed athwart the car. In the United States, open wagons for passengers were not common. Almost everyone traveled in enclosed wooden coaches of one kind or another.

By the 1880s many American passenger cars were heated by coal or wood-burning stoves. It seems that it took most European railwaymen a bit longer to understand that it did get cold in the winter; heated cars were far less common in Europe than in the United States. However, the heating stoves in railway carriages were a mixed blessing. If you sat too close to them, you were baked. If you were at the end of the car away from the stove, it may as well have not been there. For all passengers, the stove presented the very real possiblity of immolation in the event of a wreck, and wrecks were all too frequent. One advantage of the open wagon was the near impossibility of burning to death in case of an accident. Riders in those cars would likely be thrown out if there was a wreck and die quickly from a broken neck.

Another advantage of freight, as far as railway men were concerned, was that freight (other than livestock) did not have to eat or attend to functions of nature. Early trains did not have dining cars or any other kind of food service, and the concept of a lavatory on a railway car just wasn't there. Since there were usually frequent stops, such amenities were not considered to be necessary. Enterprising people soon set up food services of various descriptions at stations. These varied from vendors selling food from baskets or push-carts to large restaurants. The quality of these ventures also varied. Some earned reputations so good that people who were not railway passengers patronized them. Others were so notoriously bad as to border on the criminal. There were many instances of bribing the conductor to blow a quick departure whistle so the hapless passengers would not have time to finish their meals. The unconsumed but paid-for victuals could then be sold to the next set of victims on the following train. Stations were scenes of frenzied activity as passengers scurried about looking for a lavatory, bolted down food, or ran to make connections.

In the early days, premium-fare passengers rode in what were essentially stagecoaches with flanged wheels. These familiar vehicles may have provided a feeling of security for the apprehensive passengers. However, railwaymen soon discovered that while a team of horses could handle only one stagecoach, an improved steam locomotive could pull several carriages, any of which was much heavier than a stagecoach. For a while

railway carriages which were three or four stagecoach bodies mounted on a single four-wheel wagon frame were widely used in Europe. The European style railway coach divided into compartments evolved from this concept.

The earliest railway carriages in America also looked like stagecoaches, but the passenger cars that evolved in the United States were quite different from those in Europe. The basic design of the American passenger coach was mainly the work of a New Jersey farmer named Ross Winans who became one of the foremost railway inventors in the world. Winans knew that European railway carriages would not do on American rails. Europeans ran their railway cars on fixed wheels, which were fine for the relatively straight lines and solidly constructed railways of Europe, but not for the generally wild and primitive conditions that prevailed in North America. American railways tended to have more curves than those of Europe. The abundance of timber in North America encouraged the building of wooden trestles, while the relative scarcity of trees in England and much of the continent resulted in a greater number of iron and stone trestles in that part of the world. When fixed wheel carriages were used on American lines, derailments were frequent, particularly if there was some kind of race going on or if the engineer was just in a hurry or careless.

In attacking the problem of designing railway coaches that had a better than even chance of staying on the rails, Winans conceived the idea of mounting wheel sets at both ends of the car on a mechanism that allowed them to swivel or pivot. These free-turning wheel sets came to be known as 'trucks' in the United States and 'bogies' in England. (A coach mounted on trucks could follow curves with greater accuracy, allowing for higher speeds than could fixed wheel coaches.) As truck/bogie carriages came into wider use on North American railroads, the number of derailments decreased. The bogie concept played a significant role in the development of fast and luxurious trains, both in Europe and America.

An American train of the 1830s. The carriages owe much to stagecoach design, while the vertical boiler configuration of the locomotive proved to be one of the 'blind alleys' of mechanical engineering.

Top: Old No. 9 – *the first Pullman car. This 20-berth sleeper was 40 feet long and was made largely of wood. It had two small washrooms and was heated by wood-burning stoves.*

Above: The Pioneer, *a Pullman sleeping car built in 1865 was a great improvement, being much larger and with a high quality finish.*

Above: *George Pullman.*
Right: *Pullman's influence spread far beyond the USA. The newly-restored*

club car Barbara is seen here on the Kent & East Sussex Railway, England, in June 1984.

Winan's coaches were much longer than the stagecoach-type carriages used previously. They had platforms at each end, and rather than being divided into compartments, they featured a central aisle with seats on either side. This arrangement became the standard for American coaches, while compartment coaches continued to be the norm in Europe.

Through the first half of the nineteenth century and beyond, most railroads continued to give minimal attention to passenger service, concentrating on lucrative freight operations. Railroads were a vital component of the Industrial Revolution which rapidly created a new wealthy class that represented a potentially profitable market for railroads. Here were customers who would travel by train if they could do so in comfort, if not luxury, if they did not have to scramble like rats to get something to eat during their journey, and if they could find a place to go to the bathroom before the situation got desperate. What is more important is that they could afford to pay for all these amenities. There were even a few far-

seeing individuals who had the temerity to suggest that some people might even be willing to pay for a real bed on which they could stretch out and go to sleep on long journeys.

Above: *An American Pullman day car sleeper of the late 19th century.*

The replica of Rocket *on Britain's Bluebell Railway in 1982. The original was built by Stephenson in 1829 for the Liverpool & Manchester Railway. It featured bar frames and outside cylinders, a practice followed more in America than in Britain.*

For the most part, railroad management failed to recognize the existence of this market. It remained for a few ambitious men who had no previous experience in railroading to show that railroad companies could transport passengers in comfort and make a lot of money doing it. George M Pullman is the best known of these entrepreneurs. His name came to be synonymous with railroad luxury and elegance. Born in Brockton, New York in 1831, Pullman was, like many of the restless innovators of his time, a dabbler in many things before he found the enterprise that made his fortune. Among other things, he was a store clerk, building contractor and traveling salesman.

For a while in the late 1840s, he traveled around the country selling furniture made by his brother. The long, exhausting train rides he had to take during this time convinced him there had to be a better way. Railway lines were getting longer, particularly in America. For the most part, passengers had to endure these trips on straight-backed seats that were minimally upholstered in higher-fare classes and on hard benches in low-fare sections. A few lines had introduced 'sleeping cars' of a sort. These were equipped with tiers of bunks, which were usually nothing more than planks supplied without mattresses or linens, and were available on a first-grab, first-served basis.

In 1859, armed with money gained from a building-moving business in Chicago, Pullman set out to build a proper sleeping car. He persuaded the Chicago, Alton and St Louis Railroad to lend him two day coaches, and with the help of a carpenter, but without benefit of plans, he

By 1870 Pullman Hotel Cars provided one of the most luxurious means of travel in the world. The advertisement proclaims, 'This is decidedly the Shortest and Best Route to Omaha from all Points East.' Steel Rails, Rock Ballasted Track and Air Brakes are listed as further incentives. Fine food and wine were provided, and one definitely dressed for dinner.

remodeled the interior of the car, turning it into a sleeper. During the day, the car was filled with richly upholstered seats that were to become the hallmark of the Pullman car. At night, the seat backs could be let down to become beds. The car was first run from Bloomington, Illinois to Chicago, carrying three passengers, all of whom went to bed with their boots on.

When the Civil War started, the Union Army appropriated all the Chicago and Alton cars, putting Pullman out of business. Pullman was the right age for the Army, which is probably why he immediately went west where there was no war. He knew he couldn't make any money in the Army. He spent most of the war years in the

gold-prospecting camps of Colorado. He was smart enough to know he was not likely to make much money prospecting either, so he made a bundle selling food and supplies to the prospectors at inflated prices.

As the war began to wear itself out, Pullman returned to Chicago with the money he made in Colorado and started to build another sleeping car. This time, however, he built it from the wheels up, instead of modifying an existing car. In 1864, several months and $20,170 after he started, Pullman's first sleeper, appropriately named The Pioneer, was ready. At the time, the average cost of building a passenger car was about $4000.

Pioneer's interior finish was polished black walnut. Ornate chandeliers provided candle lighting, and the wash stands were made of solid marble. In addition to richly upholstered seats that became lower berths, hinged upper berths were folded up against the ceiling. Curtains were drawn to separate the sections of berths. Many condemned the whole arrangement as an invitation to licentiousness.

To accomodate all this luxury, Pullman made the Pioneeer about a foot wider and some two and a half inches higher than any other railroad car in the United States, and in so doing he created a number of problems for his fledgling operation. The Pioneer was too wide to get through some

station platforms and a bit high for a number of overpasses on the Chicago and Alton, not to mention most other railroads in the country. No railroad was willing to make expensive alterations to its standing facilities just to accomodate The Pioneer, now widely called 'Pullman's folly.' It seemed that Pullman was about to fade from the history books when he was saved by a national tragedy.

When Abraham Lincoln was assassinated, the State of Illinois asked the Chicago and Alton to include The Pioneer in the funeral train. The railroad had no choice but to comply, and it had to alter a few platforms and bridges to allow The Pioneer to pass. Thousands of people came out to

Although the railways of the Confederacy suffered during the Civil War, they grew elsewhere and new lines and advances in motive power became commonplace. This photograph shows Abraham Lincoln's funeral train in 1865. It is drawn by the classic American locomotive of the period, a 4-4-0, complete with cowcatcher and a spark-arresting smokestack.

The Pennsylvania Limited *at speed in 1899. It ran from New York to Chicago and ushered in the era of the luxury train in North America. The* Pennsylvania Limited *was an innovation; with a passageway, haute cuisine, private bedrooms and stock market prices telegraphed along the way.*

watch the funeral train, providing Pullman with all the publicity he needed to keep his company going. On the return trip, he provided free rides and demonstrations.

In 1867, Pullman organized his operation as the Pullman Palace Car Company. In that same year, the first transcontinental line was completed with the driving of the golden spike at Promontry Point, Utah. It did not take the most brilliant business mind to figure out that the resulting increase in the length of rail journeys would likely increase the demand for comfort during those journeys. Yet, this rather obvious conclusion did not seem to get through to many

railroad men. The directors of the Michigan Central, for example, were more than skeptical, insisting that few passengers would lay out an extra two dollars to ride and sleep in Pullman's cars. Pullman and the Michigan Central agreed to a competition in which both Pullman's sleepers and the Michigan Central's bunk cars would be run on the same train. The Michigan Central learned a hard and embarassing lesson when the bunk cars ran empty, and many passengers refused to ride on Michigan Central trains unless they could have space on a Pullman. Other railroads soon rushed to make deals with Pullman.

Pullman was not without competition in those

The success of this venture encouraged railroads to build their own dining cars. Other special cars were built, such as club cars in which men could smoke and drink (these were limited to males at first), parlor cars for socializing, and observation cars for taking in the countryside. Until 1887 the full utilization of these pleasures was somewhat limited by the difficulty of passing from one car to another, an undertaking that involved going out on the open platform and stepping over the couplers into the next car. Besides being exposed to wind-swept dust, smoke and cinders, there was the possibility of falling off the train or being crushed beween the couplers. Pullman's 1887 invention of an enclosed accordion-like passageway between cars made passing between moving

Below: *The less expensive Pullman cars featured pull-down bunk beds.*

Left: *The first Pullman sleeper car 'Old No. 9.' The photograph shows how the day seats were converted into beds and how curtains could be drawn around to give privacy.*

days. Other railroads built their own luxury cars, and other ambitious men tried to start their own luxury car companies. One of the most formidable competitors, or so it seemed, was Webster Wagner, who was backed by the powerful Vanderbilts, owners of the New York Central. By the 1920s, Wagner and others were gone. Pullman had a monopoly on the sleeping car business in the United States.

In 1867 Pullman built his first 'hotel car,' which was a sleeper car equipped with a small kitchen. Meals were served to passengers on small tables set up at their sections. A year later, Pullman built his first full dining car, the Delmonico.

The Trans-Siberian has
never been one of the
grand-luxe lines of the
world, but its enormous
distance makes it a great
achievement.

Right: *Engravings from the 1880s show some of the delights of traveling across Europe in the carriages of the Compagnie Internationale des Wagons-Lits. Like all good travel firms, it offers a hint of romance.*

Below: *Georges Nagelmackers, the enterprising Belgian who founded Wagon-Lits in 1872. By the time he died in 1905, his carriages could carry one from the Atlantic to the Pacific – the long way round, via Russia.*

cars considerably safer, and long-distance train travel much more interesting.

The first train to feature Pullman's new passageway was the Pennsylvania Limited service from New York to Chicago. The term 'Limited' told the would-be passenger that this was a very special train, and that traveling on it would cost more than taking a trip on an ordinary train. Most of the Limiteds of this era were made up entirely of Pullman or similar cars, or ones that included Pullman cars that were strictly off-limits to ordinary fare-paying passengers.

By 1898, the Pennsylvania Limited offered private bedrooms, on-board stenographers, the latest stock market prices telegraphed to stations along the train's route, and club cars where you could get a drink to ease the pain of bad news from Wall Street. The dining car menu was as varied as that of many expensive restaurants offering selections such as steaks, chops, ham, chicken, quail, oysters, clams, golden plover and blue-winged teal at an average price of 50 cents a meal.

The Pennsylvania Limited was the beginning of the era of the American luxury train. Probably the best known of these was the Twentieth Century Limited, which began service in 1902 between New York and Chicago. The Twentieth-Century originated as the Exposition Flyer, a special train running from New York to Chicago as part of the 1893 Columbian Exposition in the latter city. The publicity gained from the record 20-hour run helped the New York Central to establish the train as a regular service called the Lake Shore Limited fitted out by the Wagner Palace Car Company.

The Lake Shore Limited made the New York-Chicago run in 24 hours. This was not good enough for George H Daniels, a director of the New York Central, and he pushed for a 20-hour time. This was achieved by the turn of the century, and he appropriately renamed the faster train the Twentieth Century Limited. The Pennsylvania Limited became the Broadway Limited in 1912. These two trains were keen competitors; the New York Central and Pennsylvania Railroads spent lavishly to maintains standards of luxury and to increase speed.

A Twentieth Century passenger was made to feel special as soon as he got to the station. Starting in 1922, a six-foot wide, 260-foot long maroon welcoming carpet was laid out along the Century's departing platform at New York's Grand Central Station. The least expensive accomodation was lavish compared to ordinary train travel. This was the roomette, a small sitting room by day and a bedroom by night. By the 1940s it was equipped with a mechanism that lowered a fully-made bed from the wall at the touch of a button. For more money there were single and double bedrooms, drawing rooms and, at the top of the price list was the master room, which was a suite consisting of a two-berth bedroom, a lounge and a private bathroom equipped with a shower.

Other crack trains of this era were the Merchant's Limited of the New York, New Haven and Hartford, Southern Pacific's Daylight and Santa Fe's Chief and Super Chief. In Canada luxurious coast-to-coast service was provided on trains such as The Dominion, Confederation, and Continental Limited. One of the most lavish of the American special trains was the New York and Florida Special, later called simply the Florida Special. Launched in 1888 by Henry Flagler, this was a winter-only, all-Pullman service running over the lines of several railroads including Flagler's own Florida East Coast Line. The idea was to promote tourism in Florida, particularly among those Americans wealthy enough to spend their winters in coastal resorts. It made the 1074-mile trip from New York to Jacksonville in 30 hours. The final destination was close to Flagler's lavish, pseudo-Moorish Hotel Ponce de Leon in St Augustine. In the inaugural weeks the dining car menu included offerings such as salmon à la Chambourg, fricandeau of veal à la Richelieu, roast saddle of antelope, and salmi of duck à la

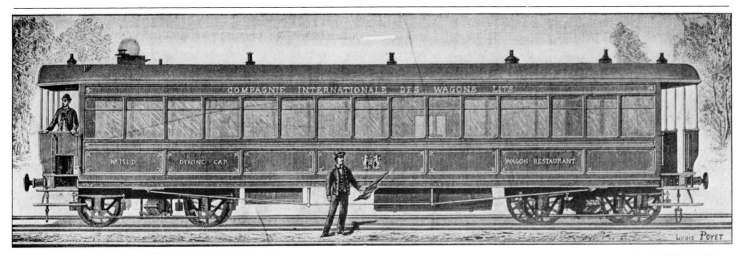

A 2-6-0 locomotive on a section of the Trans-Siberian Railway controled by Italian forces supporting the 'Whites' during the Russian Civil War. Given the poor state of the roads and the vast distances, command of the railways was of vital strategic importance to both the Bolsheviks and the counter-revolutionaries.

Jardiniere. The price of a full meal was about one dollar. In 1926, a recreation car was added in which there were games in the daytime and dancing to a small band at night. The Florida Special's successors managed to compete with airlines for a while in the 1960s with such attractions as complimentary champagne to go with the candle-lit dinner and bathing suit fashion shows in the lounge car.

What was happening in Europe while Pullman was building his empire in the United States? A few European lines experimented with sleeping cars as early as the 1830s. Ross Winans designed a sleeper for Russia's Nicolai Railway. This car included a small spiral staircase between a double-decker lounge section. But the political situation in Europe discouraged long-distance through sleeper service. Railways were regarded as military asssets. They ended at borders, and neighboring countries' lines were occasionally of a different gauge, a situation that necessitated changing trains if you wanted to travel across the border. Couplers were not standard. This was fine as far as the military was concerned; they did not want railways to be a fast way for an enemy to move troops across borders. The first international train in Europe was run in 1863 from Basel to Rotterdam. It happened only because several large European banking houses reinforced diplomatic pressure with offers of investment capital to the various railways involved.

The mover behind the initiation of international luxury service in Europe was George Nagelmackers, a Belgian engineer and scion of a rich Belgian banking family. In 1863, when he was 23 years old, his parents sent him on a trip to America to ease the scandal of a none-too-discreet

affair with an older woman. During this trip, he was greatly impressed with Pullman's operation. He immediately saw the need for a similar service in Europe, fully aware that international rivalries and suspicions would make its establishment very difficult.

In 1870 he returned to Europe and started to make plans while working for a mining company. The Franco-Prussian War of 1870 delayed the project, as did the stony attitudes of railway management and recalcitrant governments. Yet by 1872 he had set up his Compagnie Internationale de Wagons Lits, and had entered into contracts with railways in Holland and Belgium allowing him to run his sleeping cars between Cologne and Ostend. Later, he entered into contracts with German railroads to run sleepers from Vienna to Munich and from Ostend to Berlin. Pullman built his cars as he saw fit, but Nagelmackers had to make them according to the railway's specifications. However, like Pullman, his first sleepers were converted day coaches. He converted four small 4-wheeled cars from Austria, but the Germans insisted on 6-wheel cars. As was the case in most of Europe at the time, these were fixed wheel carriages. Seat backs formed beds, and upper berths were lowered by rope and pulley from the ceiling.

Response to the first service opened in 1873 was not particularly enthusiastic. Nagelmacker's own family refused to finance him further. He was bailed out by an opportunistic American, Colonel William d'Alton Mann. In contrast to Pullman, Mann had served in the Army during the American Civil War, and he made money from his Army experience. He designed a number of items of military equipment during and after his

Army tenure, obtaining patents on them all. With the help of old Army buddies, he sold most of them to the American military. With the money he made, he tried to enter the luxury car business in the United States in competition with Pullman, counting on his patented sleeper car that featured individual compartments rather than Pullman's sections. He was unable to compete with Pullman, so he went to England where he met Nagelmackers. In 1873 the two men formed a partnership called Mann's Railway Sleeping Carriage Company, registered in London. The company ran sleeping cars called Mann's Boudoir Sleeping Cars.

Mann was a good salesman, and he mananged to get contracts with two railways in France that Nagelmackers had been unable to convince. Mann also talked the Prince of Wales into using a 'boudoir car' for a long trip that took him through Berlin on a trip to St Petersburg, a trip that served to make international train travel fashionable among Europe's high society. With the help of this publicity, Nagelmackers was able to establish a successful Paris-Vienna service.

Nagelmackers was able to buy out Mann in 1876, and to reorganize the operation as Compagnie Internationale des Wagons-Lits et des Grands Express Europeens, more generally referred to as the Wagons-Lits Company or the International Sleeping Car Company. The major stockholder was Leopold II, King of all the Belgians.

By 1880, Nagelmackers had added dining car service, although various German companies obtained catering concessions for trains running through that country. Closed vestibules and car-to-car passage also came in that year, as did the first 8-wheel bogied sleeping car in Europe. The latter development eventually led to technical innovations that made higher speeds possible.

Pullman started operations in Europe in the mid-1870s. James Allport, manager of Britain's Midland Railway, was impressed with Pullman's

Civilians wait to board the Trans-Siberian Express at Kharbin in 1920.

operation and entered into contracts with him to run his cars on the Midland. Pullman's cars provided British rail passengers with a degree of luxury and comfort they had not known before, as well as a number of other firsts. Pullman cars were among the first passenger cars on trucks in the UK, and the first to have lavatories in ordinary first- and second-class coaches, a corridor and central hot-water heating. Pullman also gave Britain its first dining car and its first parlor car, equipped with individual swiveling arm chairs. Regular service from London to Bradford began on 1st June 1874. Later in the year, Pullman won a contract with two railways in northern Italy.

In 1881 the London, Brighton and South Coast Railway started an all-Pullman day service from London to Brighton, later called the Southern Belle. The success of this luxury service encouraged a number of similar express services in Britain.

Britain and Italy were the only European countries in which Pullman gained contracts. By 1880, he had only a dozen or so cars on the continent and some 40 in Britain, compared to Nagelmackers' 100 plus. That disparity did not deter the audacious Pullman from proposing a fifty-fifty merger with Wagons-Lits, an offer understandably rebuffed by Nagelmackers. Pullman's Italian operations were bought out by Wagons-Lits in 1885, a move that enabled Nagelmackers to establish the Rome Express, a luxury service from London to Rome via Calais in 1871. Because Pullman had the north Italian contracts, Nagelmackers had been unable to run cars on a direct route to Italian destinations. Shortly after Nagelmackers turned down the merger offer, Pullman had given Nagelmackers a bit of a scare when he worked out a deal with Thomas Cook to run a special Pullman train from Calais to Rome for an art exhibition. Nagelmackers was rather upset because the route of this special train included French lines with which he had had exclusive contracts to run sleeper cars. Actually, Pullman conceived of the deal as a way to cover the cost of transferring five underused sleepers from England to Italy. It never happened again.

Wagons-Lits got to Russia in 1892 with service to St Petersburg. These trains frequently carried Russian and Austrian royalty and nobility along with their servants. Full evening dress was the norm in the dining cars. Russian service was later extended in a train called the Trans-Siberian Express, an overland route to China. The wide Russian loading gauge allowed for the building of particularly luxurious sleeping cars, diners and lounge cars, all of which would have been very welcome on the long (nine days in 1904) trip. Although these luxurious cars were displayed at the Paris Exposition of 1900, they never made it to regular service on the Trans-Siberian Express.

The success of the Paris-Vienna service encouraged Nagelmackers to extend it to eastern Europe. The result was Nagelmackers' tour-de-force – the Orient Express – the most famous of luxury trains.

The Coming of Speed

Today when we think of fast trains, what is most likely to come to mind are 'streamlined' diesel or electric locomotives. It is true that none of today's superfast trains are hauled by a steam locomotive. Most are electrically powered, and a few are pulled by diesel locomotives. However, by the turn of the century some steam locomotives were regularly attaining speeds greater than that of some of today's trains. While most super high-speed trains have an appearance that can be accurately described as streamlined, many of the fast locomotives of this century (100 mph and above) were rather boxy in appearance. Streamlining was as much a design phenomenon as a technological one, extending beyond transportation into design of everyday items such as toasters, furniture, telephones and electric razors.

By the last quarter of the nineteenth century, public railways had been in existence for 50 years. They were no longer a novelty, and most passengers paid the price of a ticket to get from one place to another as quickly as possible in reasonable comfort, not for the thrill of riding the train. Accordingly, railway management began to look for ways to make their trains faster than the competition's. One of the first speed competitions began around 1875 in Great Britain. The Midland Railway, whose route ran through the center of the British Island, announced a cut in fares. The only response London and North Western (which ran the west coast route) could muster was reducing the time of its lunch stops from 30 minutes to 20 minutes. The East Coast line decided to go for increased speed, and by 1880 it was, in all probability, the fastest railway in the world, averaging 54 mph on its London-Manchester and London-Leeds expresses. At first, the West Coast line was not worried. The East Coast railways did not carry third-class passengers, leaving that lucrative segment of business almost exclusively to the West Coast, who continued to run their trains as slowly as they pleased. However, in 1887 when the East Coast line announced that it would start to carry third-class passengers on its fast King's Cross-Edinburgh service, the West Coast Railways, fearing they would lose all their third-class passengers to the faster service, were moved to action. Thus began the 'races to the north,' the great East Coast-West Coast speed wars of the 1880s and 1890s.

In June of 1888 the West Coast announced a cut of an hour in its London to Glasgow and Edinburgh trains, accomplished this time by increased speed instead of by an attack on passengers' digestive systems. The East Coast parried with a reduction of running time to Edinburgh

A London to Glasgow express, double-headed for the climb up Camden Bank.

A North British 4-4-2 pulls a passenger train across the second Tay Bridge, on the line between Edinburgh and Dundee. The original bridge collapsed in 1879 while a train was crossing, with the loss of 78 lives.

that made its London-Edinburgh 11 minutes faster than that of the West.

The war intensified with the completion of the Firth and Tay bridges that gave the East Coast lines a record-breaking three-hour advantage over the West Coast Line. The West Coast responded with the innovation of a shallow water trough that allowed locomotives to scoop up water while running, thus reducing the number of water stops. Speeds in excess of 75 mph were now practical and safe.

The British speed wars encouraged the development of faster train service elsewhere in Europe and in North America. American railways took the British achievements as a challenge, one which led to the Twentieth Century Limited and other fast service in the 1890s and 1900s. A speed of 112.5 mph was claimed for a short stretch on the Empire State Express run, a precursor of the Twentieth Century Limited, on 9 May 1893. In a later confession, the speed was downgraded to 90 mph, still an impressive speed at that time.

Increased speeds of steam locomotives were achieved through a number of technical innovations, such as increasing the diameter of driving wheels, coupling the driving wheels, compounding, and bogied front wheels. Also important were improvements in tracks and signaling. Pullman's inter-car crossings helped to keep the cars in line during high speeds.

While steam locomotive technology continued to advance well into the twentieth cen-

tury, their speed and performance were limited by basic principles of thermodynamics as they applied to external combustion engines such as steam locomotives. High speeds came with internal combustion engines – diesel, gasoline and turbos – but super high speed is the domain of the electric locomotive.

A peculiar little wheeled vehicle that pulled passengers around a circular track on an open-bench car at the 1879 Berlin exhibition was the beginning of electric locomotives. Hardly three feet long and about two feet high, the peculiar vehicle was indeed an electric locomotive. The motorman sat on top of the contrivance, somewhat like a child sitting on toy rollabout. That funny-looking little vehicle was the beginning of a technological revolution that eventually resulted in today's fast super trains.

By 1883, the first public electric railway had been started. Still in operation today, Volk's Electric Railway runs along the shore at the English seaside resort town of Brighton. The single electric cars of Volk's Electric railway ran on low voltage electric current fed to two 8 hp motors. Low voltage direct current (DC) was fine for short distances, but was less economic for long distances. Direct current does not travel well. Transmission of DC over long distances requires booster stations along the way to keep it going. Of course, these booster stations add to the expense of constructing the line. However, DC was popu-

lar because the locomotives that ran on it were simpler and less expensive to build than those than ran on alternating current.

Alternating current (AC) travels well over long distances, but as might be expected, AC locomotives are more complex and expensive than DC locomotives. The battle over the relative merits, or lack of merit, of the two systems was fairly vigorous in the years around the turn of the century. Direct current prevailed as long as it did only because its chief champion was Thomas Edison. Alternating current was promoted by Edison's arch rival George Westinghouse. Alternating current eventually won out for many applications of long-range transmisssion. Today,

Volk's Electric Railway was the first permanent public line driven by electric traction. It opened in Brighton, England, in 1883.

England's Great Western Railway is one of the legends of the Age of Steam. Built, in part, by the great engineer Isambard Kingdom Brunel, it ran from London to the West Country and Wales. Brunel built the line on the Broad-Gauge of 5 ft 6 in; as opposed to the Standard-Gauge of 4 ft 8½ in first used by Stephenson himself. This photograph shows the last Broad-Gauge train leaving Paddington Station, London, before the GWR's conversion to the standard-gauge used by the other main routes.

the battle seems somewhat academic. There is a veritable arsenal of technology that allows direct current locomotives to be used on alternating current lines and vice versa. Another problem is that the voltage needed for transmission of AC is too high for efficiently running electric locomotive motors. Today, on-board electrical equipment converts AC to DC, reduces the voltage as required, and makes adjustments for different voltages and frequencies (cycles per second, or cps or Hertz [Hz]) encountered as a train goes from one country to another. In the early days, this was not always expedient, as the necessary equipment was cumbersome and heavy. Many railways constructed their own power stations and transmission lines. The development of mercury arc rectifiers and solid state electronics led the way to the development of the fast, lightweight electric locomotives and trains of today.

Around the turn of the century, a great deal of engineering effort was directed toward designing electric locomotives that operated directly on the frequencies supplied by commercial power to run three-phase AC motors. An industrial consortium in Germany, the *Studiengesellschaft fur Elektrisch Schnellbahner* (Study Group for High Speed Railways) was formed to study ways of making fast electric locomotives. In 1901 two 50-seat electric railcars fitted with 1000 hp traction motors were assembled and taken to a 14-mile long military

railway near Berlin. In the first trials, the cars achieved 75 mph, but they lurched and rolled violently. The electrical transmission wires had been placed to the side rather than overhead, and as the cars swayed and lurched, contact with the wires was alternately broken, causing intense arcing very much like lightning. A speed of more than 100 mph was achieved, but at this speed one of the bogies actually bounced off the track and back again, damaging the track.

The track was repaired, and the bogies were modified and they tried again in 1903. This time a speed of 130.5 mph was achieved without damaging track, bogies, cars or people. In spite of this triumph, there was no rush for three-phase AC electrification. However, there was a rapid conversion to lower frequency electrification, single-phase in Switzerland and three-phase in Italy.

In the first two decades of the twentieth century, it seemed that all of North American Railroads would eventually be electrified. The first mainline electrification in the United States was completed in 1895. It ran through and under Baltimore, and was built only because the Baltimore city fathers ordered the Baltimore and Ohio to stop running steam locomotives in the city. The electric locomotives hooked on to the trains, steam locomotive and all (with its fire banked), and pulled it through the streets and tunnels of the city. The tunnel under Park Avenue in New

This photograph, taken in 1926, shows the Southern Railway's Atlantic Express leaving Waterloo Station, Sir Calacars (one of the more obscure knights of King Arthur's Round Table) shows the classic lines of a thoroughbred locomotive.

York's Grand Central Terminal was electrified with a third-rail system in 1902, but only after a tragic accident, caused by smoke-obscured signals.

One of the most ambitious early American electrifications was completed by the New York, New Haven and Hartford in 1907. This was a single-phase 15 cycle, 11,000V catenary (overhead wire) system from Woodlawn, just north of New York, to Stamford. It was later extended to New Haven. The Great Northern electrified a section of its track in the Cascade Mountains after passengers choked on coal fumes in the 2.6 mile long Cascade Tunnel. The Chicago, Milwaukee and St Paul put hundreds of miles of track in the Rocky and Cascade mountains under the wires in the 1910s. The last great railway electrification project in the United States was completed by the Pennsylvania Railroad in 1933, putting its main tracks east of Harrisburg under the wires. When it was finished, electric locomotives could be run from Washington, DC to New Haven. American railway management then seemed to lose interest in electrification. At the time, coal was cheap and plentiful in the United States, as was oil, a factor that contributed to the rapid dieselization of railways after World War II.

In most of Europe, electrification was eagerly adopted. In France, the most productive coal fields had been severely damaged in the war.

Labor unrest after the war did not improve the situation. Switzerland's mountains with their flowing rivers and streams promised an abundance of relatively cheap hydroelectric power, and virtually all that country's railways were electrified within ten years of end of World War I. The Simplon Tunnel, finished in 1906, was equipped with a 3kV, three-phase, 15Hz system, allowing electric locomotives to haul the Simplon Orient Express through that leg of its journey

In Italy, Mussolini was determined to make his country's technology better than anyone else's. A massive railway electrification project was near the top of the Italian dictator's priority list. Italy's railways had been regarded as among the worst in the world. One traveled on them only if it was absolutely necessary. Il Duce was determined to make Italian railways second to none, and he did, indeed, make Italian trains run on time. In addition to rapidly electrifying the existing Italian railways, two new lines, the *Direttissime*, were constructed. These lines, one between Rome and Naples and the other running from Bologna to Florence, dramatically shortened travel time between these cities. Just before the start of World War I the best one could hope for on a trip between Rome and Naples was about 17 grueling hours. By 1939 the trip took only eight hours.

Until the 1930s and 1940s, Il Duce's quest for

Left: British steam at its peak. This 1932 photograph shows LNER's Flying Scotsman leaving London's King's Cross Station for the North.

Below: In complete contrast is the Zeppelin company's propeller-driven railcar designed by Dr Ing Franz Kruchenberg, pictured here in 1931.

Union Pacific's City of Salina was the original American streamliner. First seen at Chicago's Century of Progress Exposition in 1934, it was later put into service between that city and Salina over Burlington's rails.

George Bennie's 'rail plane' was an innovative system tested for Glasgow but not put into practice.

proceeded rapidly after 1939, slowed only by World War II. By the end of the 1940s, orders for new steam locomotives in North America had all but stopped, and before the 1950s were over the Age of Steam was done, at least in North America.

Most locomotives called diesels are actually electric locomotives carrying their own power source. The diesel engines turn electric dynamos or generators, producing current for electric motors that drive the wheels. As such they are more correctly referred to as self-generating electric locomotives. Of course the engine that supplies the power to turn the dynamo does not have to be a diesel. Some of the earliest self-generating locomotives were powered by gasoline engines. A small company in La Grange, Illinois, the Electromotive Company, started to manufacture

Union Pacific's City of Portland featured a style later to be seen on the bullet trains of Japan.

speed was not shared by most other people running railways. Electric traction was regarded as just a way to cut costs and provide the power that was needed to get trains over mountain grades and through tunnels without asphyxiating the passengers. However, as airplanes and automobiles became more competitive, railways had to start giving more thought to speed. Electrification was one way to achieve super speeds on railways. However, the electric locomotive had a formidable competitor, particularly in North America, in the form of locomotives powered by diesel and other kinds of internal combustion engines.

The embracing of diesels by railways, particularly those of North America, was so fast that it was practically complete before anyone knew what had happened. The first diesel locomotive used in main line service was on the rails of the Canadian National in 1928. Conversion to diesel

small gasoline-electric railcars in 1927. These were single passenger cars containing their own source of motive power. They were generally called doodlebugs.

In 1930, Electromotive and the Winton Company that supplied engines for Electromotive were bought by General Motors. This transaction was the beginning of what could be called the Streamliner Era. General Motors supplied the money and experience for Electromotive to build an all-Pullman, three-car, articulated, aluminum train for Union Pacific. Designated the M-10000, its source of power was a V-12 gasoline engine. The M-10000 was a *trainset*. That is, the power car was integrated with the rest of the train. You could not detach the locomotive from the cars.

In 1934, the M-10000 went on a 12,000-mile coast-to-coast tour, demonstrating a capability for 100 mph speeds at several points along the way. Millions of people, including President

Mallard is the holder of the World Speed Record for steam traction. In 1938 the LNER A4 Pacific, designed by Sir Nigel Gresley, achieved the speed of 126 mph.

Franklin D Roosevelt, came out to see the stream-lined M-10000, as it went through more than 60 cities in its way to the 1934 Century of Progress Exhibition in Chicago.

When the M-10000 got to the Exhibition, it had to compete for attention with another streamliner, the Burlington's three-car articulated train-set, The Pioneer Zephyr. Powered by 600 hp diesel engine, the Pioneer Zephyr went directly from Denver to Chicago, a 1015 mile trip it completed in just under 13 hours and five minutes, for an average speed of 77.6 mph. The Burlington's accountants were no doubt pleased that the train consumed only 418 gallons of diesel fuel (the price of diesel fuel was about 15 cents a gallon in 1934). The M-10000 ran in regular service as the City of Salina.

It would seem that 1934, one of the worst years of the Great Depression, was hardly the time to introduce a new line of fast, luxurious trains. However, the time turned out to be most propitious. The public's fascination with streamlining had been excited by the work of designers such as Raymond Loewy and Norman Bel Geddes. The streamlining concept had come to mean much more than just a way to cut down air resistance on moving vehicles. Streamlined design was the symbol of a beautiful new age of prosperity over the horizon, in which sleek, shiny, silvery, streamlined trains streaked between gleaming steel and concrete cities. The streamliner was an expression of hope that as bad as things were, technology would make it all right again.

Makers of steam locomotives tried to keep up with the times by streamlining their locomotives.

While many of these locomotives were well designed and some were quite fast, they could not hope to compete with diesel and electric. The record for a steam engine is held by a British A4 Pacific streamlined locomotive. Mallard designed by Sir Nigel Gresley reached 126 mph in 1938. But a German electric railcar had achieved over 130 mph just 35 years earlier. The diesel record was set by a British train in 1973. However, diesel-powered trains cannot reach the speeds obtained by the fastest of today's high speed electric trains.

Later in 1934, the Union Pacific built another six-car streamlined train, the M-100001. This train cut the previous best coast-to-coast time by some 14 hours. It ran as the City of Portland between Chicago and Portland. The Burlington was so pleased with the Pioneer Zephyr that it ordered more and made them bigger. Twelve-car sets ran between Chicago and Denver as the Denver Zephyrs starting in 1936. A shortened version of the Denver Zephyr set a new speed record on 23 October 1936. It completed a Chicago-Denver run at an average speed of 83.3 mph, reaching a top speed of 116 mph. This record still stands for trips of more than 1000 miles. The remarkable thing about this record-setting trip was that it was from east to west; it had to climb the some 5000 feet from the plains up to the Mile-High City.

In addition to being technological wonders, the Citys and the Zephyrs were financially successful, booked to capacity on most of their runs. Their success encouraged other railways to look at the possibility of adding their own lines of fast streamliners. German efforts at fast streamliners began in 1933 with the introduction of the two-car Fliegende Hamburger (Flying Hamburger). This light-weight, diesel-powered streamliner ran from Berlin to Hamburg at an average speed of 77.4 mph. Following its success, there were other Fliegendes, the Fliegende Kollner and the Fliegende Frankfurter. Three-car and four-car sets followed, linking most major German cities. These trains were the first to attain an average speed of 80 mph on regular runs.

French high-speed diesel sets included some rather strange beasts such as the Michelin railcar which had rubber tires on its flanged wheels. Bugatti two-car sets with top speeds of about 100 mph were introduced in 1934. The engineer of the Bugatti train did his work in a raised observation dome in the center that gave him an excellent view of the track ahead, but he could not see the front of the train. At this time, these trains could not reach their full potential because of French laws limiting the speed of trains. However, the French did up the limit from 75 mph to 90 mph to partially accomodate the capabilities of these trains.

In Britain, the Coronation Express from London to York was Britain's fastest pre-war train at an average speed of 71.9 mph. Other pre-war British streamliners included the West Riding

Limited from London to Leeds, and the London-Glasgow Coronation Scot.

In the United States, most of the fast luxury trains were diesel-powered. Exceptions included trains running on electrified sections of the Northeast Corridor between Washington and New Haven served by the Pennsylvania Railroad and the New York, New Haven and Hartford Railroad. At New Haven, the electric locomotive was replaced by a steam locomotive of the old

Below: *The Royal Scot. The LMS express competed with the Flying Scotsman as the prestige express train from London to Scotland.*

Bottom: *Another of Gresley's A4 Pacific's Silver Link leaves Kings Cross in 1935.*

days, and by a diesel today for the rest of the run to Boston. The Chicago, Milwaukee and St Paul changed its electrified lines in the West to diesel in 1974. The Northeast Corridor remains the only major long-distance electrified line in the United States. However, the PR and the NY, NH and H have passed into history.

The most familiar locomotive to those who traveled the Northeast Corridor anytime from the mid 1930s to just a few years ago, was the fabled GG1. Designed by Raymond Loewy, 139 of these powerful and dependable electric locomotives were built for the PR. Rated at 4390 hp (3680 kV), the GG1 could muster 8500 hp (6340 kV) for short bursts. Capable of 100 mph, a GG1 could easily haul a 20-car train without a suggestion of being overworked. When the PR went bankrupt, the GG1s were parceled out to its various successors, including Penn-Central, Conrail, and Amtrak. A few were still in operation in the 1980s.

The Atchison, Topeka and Santa Fe helped to assure the future of diesel traction in the United States by choosing diesels to haul the Super Chief starting in 1936, setting a regular schedule of 39 hours and 45 minutes for the 2277-mile trip. At about the same time, the Electromotive Company decided to start making production units rather than building to specification for each customer. The E series started in 1937, and the F series introduced in 1939, soon became the most commonly seen locomotives on American rails, and similar models were made for those of many other countries. These could be purchased with cabs and streamlined front ends, or in boxy-looking cabless units. These units could be joined in any number of combinations to meet different requirements of load, terrain and so on. The American Locomotive Company's PA series had a longer snout than the E or F but most people couldn't tell them apart.

The Elecromotive GP series was introduced in 1949. Also called road switchers or load units, these versatile machines could be used for both yard and main-line work. Visibility on these non-streamlined locomotives is much better than that offered by most of the streamlined diesel locomotives used in the United States and Canada.

After World War II, passenger rail service in the United States fell on hard times. American railways could not effectively compete for passengers with faster airplanes, and highways built with government money. They were also hampered by government regulations dating from the Robber Baron era after the Civil War, when the then powerful railroads were perceived as a threat.

European railways also suffered from competition with airplanes and highways. However, in spite of massive war destruction, they were in a better position to handle this competition than were their counterparts in North America. In most European countries, railways were owned and run by the government and received government subsidies. Railways were as much objects of national pride as ways to make money. Distances between major European cities were not as great as in the United States, thus reducing the incentive to choose air travel. A substantial nucleus of electrified lines had been completed before the war. Filling in the gaps proceeded rapidly in the post-war years, paving the way for the fast super trains that were to come.

A sampling of the speeds that could be attained with electric traction was provided by the French

France has always been at the forefront of locomotive design.
Above: A CC7100 electric hauls an express past Lake Bourget in Savoy during the 1950s.
Right and below right: Ettore Bugatti is remembered largely for his superlative sports and racing cars. Le Pur Sang (thoroughbred) is an apt description of his products. His diesel railcar was to be seen on French lines in the 1930s.

National Railways – *Societe Nationale des Chemins de Fer Francais* (SNCF) – in a series of tests carried out in the early 1950s with a class CC7100 locomotive. The CC7100 Class electric locomotives were ordered for the electrified Paris-Lyon line. These machines boasted a number of significant improvements in the design of the bogies or trucks that greatly enhanced stability and safety at very high speeds. By 1954, these locomotives had set impressive 77.1 mph average speeds, hauling 650 tons. This locomotive was then chosen for tests intended to determine the effects of very high speed on locomotives, track, pantographs and other factors.

The tests began in 1953. On a level stretch of track between Dijon and Beaune, a CC 7100 locomotive pulling a 111-ton train achieved a speed of 151 mph. This broke the previous record of 143 mph set in 1929 by an interesting German railcar equipped with a rear-mounted propellor. A target speed of 300 kmh (185 mph) was set for the next series of tests, carried out in 1955. A CC 7100 fitted with special high-ratio gears pulling a three-car train reached the target speed in 13 miles, and maintained it for another 7.5 miles. Then the speed increased to 330.8 kmh (205.6 mph) for about 1¼ miles; the CC7100 became the first locomotive to go faster than 200 mph. As if that were not enough, a BB 9004 locomotive repeated the performance the next day. As of this writing, this record still stands for locomotives, although some types of railcars have surpassed it.

Le Pur Sang du Rail

L'AUTOMOTRICE RAPIDE BUGATTI

The Orient Express

When George Nagelmackers inaugurated his luxury Paris-Vienna-Constantinople service, the Orient Express in 1883, he could have been accused of perpetrating a fraud. It was not possible to run a train between Vienna and Constantinople in 1883. A line between these two cities had never been completed; there were just too many powerful interests opposed to it.

The idea of a railway that would link Constantinople to the rest of Europe did not originate with Nagelmackers. In 1869, one Baron Maurice de Hirsch obtained a concession from the Sultan of the Ottoman Turkish Empire to construct a railway eastward from Constantinople through the Balkan Peninsula, most of which was still under Turkish control at the time. This venture was called the Chemins de Fer Orienteaux (Oriental Railway Company). However, Russia did not want a direct rail link between Turkey – its almost constant enemy – and the rest of Europe, particularly Austria and Germany. So the Russians helped the Bulgarians to revolt against the Turks, a bit of international intrigue that was highly successful. The newly established Bulgarian nation then did all it could to prevent the completion of Hirsch's railway.

The British were also not particularly happy at the prospect of a trans-European rail service that might take business away from their shipping interests, so they too plotted and schemed to keep central European rail lines in as fragmented a state as they could manage. This was rather ironic, as British tourists – businessmen, diplomats, not to mention spies – became some of the most frequent riders on the Orient Express.

Many observers predicted that the Orient Express would attract few passengers because it had to pass through the Balkan Peninsula. At the time few western Europeans went there because the area was considered to be dangerous. Internecine warfare, almost tribal in nature, was constant, and bandits freely roamed the countryside.

The route of the earliest versions of the Orient Express ran from Paris to Munich, Salzburg, Vienna, Budapest, Bucharest and on to Girgiu, a small city on the Rumanian side of the Danube. At Girgiu the passengers had to leave the luxury of the Wagons-Lits cars and take a ferry across the Danube to the Bulgarian town of Ruschuk (now Ruse). There the passengers were met by stony, cool, correct Russians and Bulgarians who watched them warily as they boarded a train that took them to Varna, a port on the Black Sea. This section of the route was based on a very fragile agreement Nagelmackers had worked out with the Bulgarians, one which could be terminated at

The elegant dining car on the modern Venice Simplon Orient Express.

The St Gotthard tunnel through the Swiss Alps was opened in 1882. The engraving shows the arrival of the inaugural train at Arrolo at the southern end of the tunnel.

a moment's notice. At Varna, they boarded a steamer that took them to Constantinople via the Black Sea and the Bosporus.

When the passengers set out on their journey from Paris they thought the train was going to take them directly to Constantinople; no one told them otherwise. It seems that all the changes of conveyance did not upset most of the passengers. They knew they were making history. Actually, the route Naglemackers arranged for the inaugural run was far more preferable to the other choice, the one Nagelmackers had to use on subsequent runs until 1888. This route went from Budapest to Belgrade and then to a town called Nis. From Nis, the passengers had to travel on stagecoaches over bone-shaking, rutted paths that passed for roads in the Balkans to a railhead in a place called Tatar Pazadjik, where they boarded the train that took them to Constantinople. The amazing thing is that these coaches were never robbed, even though they passed through areas known to be infested with bandits. The reputations of some of the coachmen for ferocity probably helped to keep the bandits away. However, this same ferocity was applied to passengers who often had to push the coaches through mud. The train itself, however, *was* robbed in 1891.

A truly international train linking Constantinople with western Europe was a dream Nagel-

mackers nurtured even before the founding of the Wagons-Lits Company. Turning this dream into a reality was a far more formidable challenge than was the establishment of his original routes through France, Belgium and Germany. Complicated agreements had to be worked out with an amazing variety of governments and railway companies.

Nagelmackers had a powerful ally in the person of Leopold II, King Of All The Belgians. Leopold became a major stockholder in Wagons-Lits, and this was only one of many business interests to which he devoted far more time than he did to his kingly duties. A notorious womanizer, and regarded as somewhat of a scoundrel, Leopold provided Nagelmackers with some strategic contacts. The Archduke Joseph of Austria-Hungary was his father-in-law and Queen Victoria was his aunt.

Although Leopold helped by dropping a favorable word here and there to a royal relative, business associate or well-situated amour, Nagelmackers did all the necessary negotiating and bribing himself. The list of contracted railways included: the Est Railway of France, Alsace Lorraine Railways of Germany, State Railways of the Grand Duchy of Baden, the Kingdom of Wurtemberg State Railways, Rumanian Railways, the Imperial and Austrian State Railways Company, and the Imperial and Royal Management for the

Operations of the State Railways (Austria).

A trial run was made on 5 June 1883, but the real inaugural, the maiden voyage, was a well-publicized demonstration run that departed Paris on 4 October 1883 with Nagelmackers on board. Included on the guest list were various diplomats, financiers and government officials, and a few well-known journalists and authors. Nagelmackers reasoned correctly that their writings would prove to be very effective advertising. Among these was the French novelist Edmond About, who wrote a book about the trip. This work was the first of many on the Orient Express, both fiction and nonfiction, in various media including books, articles, plays and films.

About, widely regarded as a man of taste, was lavish in his description of the train's interior and amenities. He described mahogany and teak paneling, and armchairs covered in soft Spanish leather. Damask drapes were held back by silk cords and tassels of gold thread. The beds were covered with silk sheets. Lavatories were equipped with fixtures of Italian marble and porcelain. There was a servant stationed by the door whose sole function was to clean the lavatory after each use.

The bogie dining car helped the waiters serve without spilling a single drop of wine, soup, sauce or anything else. The dining car was illuminated by gas chandeliers which cast a soft glow on the figures of Greek gods and goddesses painted on the ceiling and on the tables set with solid silver flatware, gold-rimmed porcelain plates and Baccarat crystal. The waiters wore tail coats, breeches with silk stockings, and powdered wigs. The wigs were discontinued after a passenger complained of powder in his soup.

The ten-course meal started with soup and hors d'oeuvres (lobster, oysters, caviar), followed by fish, a gigot of game, capon, and ended with cakes, sorbets, baskets of fruit and a wide selection of cheeses.

The trip was not without a few problems. A 'hot box' developed on one of the dining car axles, probably because the extra weight of all the fine food and wines, and attempts at high speeds where the track permitted produced excess friction on the wheel bearings. The axle got red hot; black smoke and the smell of burning grease permeated the car. Nagelmackers had looked ahead to the possibility of problems such as these. Extra diners and sleepers were stationed at various points along the route. A new diner was picked up in Munich.

At major stations, the train was met by military bands and groups of dignitaries. In Vienna the passengers were regaled with a champagne supper in the station restaurant, after which they traveled in imperial coaches to see an exhibition of a new wonder – electric lighting. Vienna was all the more notable because two women, the only ladies to make the trip, boarded there. At the time, night travel on trains by unescorted women was considered to be dangerous and somewhat scandalous. These women were not exactly unescorted; they were sisters, and one was the wife of an official who had boarded in Paris. Nevertheless, their presence on the train helped

Georges Nagelmackers (seated) and William d'Alton Mann amalgamated their companies in 1876, with the former taking control of Compagnie Internationale des Wagons-Lits et des Grands Express Européans.

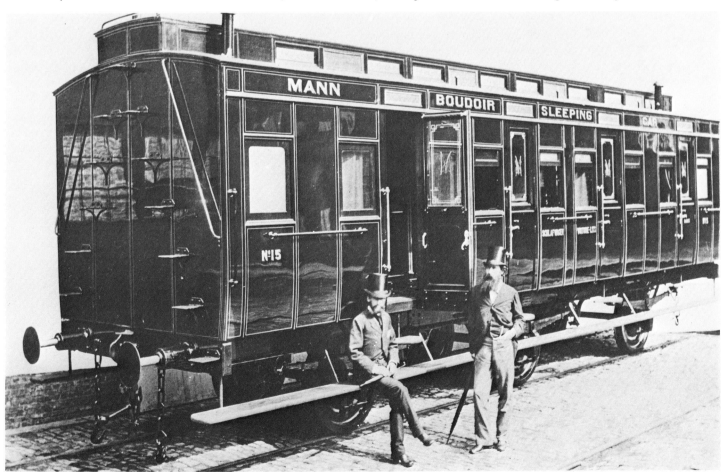

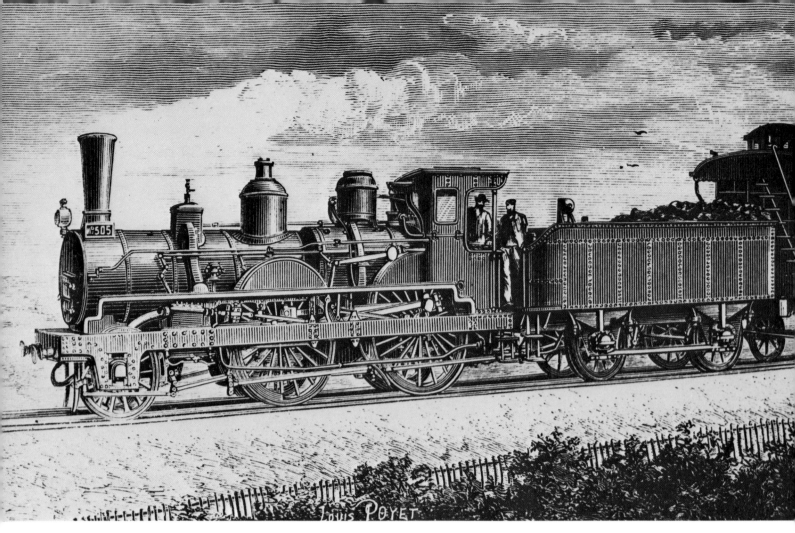

The Orient Express in 1883, the year it began operation between Paris and Constantinople (Istanbul). It crossed no less than seven national and four German state boundaries.

to make overnight train travel by women more acceptable.

In Hungary, a band of gypsies complete with tambourines, fiddles and flutes, was invited to come aboard and entertain the passengers. Tables and chairs were moved in the dining car to improvise a theater and the gypsies played and sang almost continuously. At one point they played a rather wheezy rendition of the *Marseillaise*, moving the chef to such patriotic fervor that he sang sonorously with his hand over his heart and his high chef's togue pushed back on his head.

Charles I, the sullen and morose King of Rumania, invited the passengers to visit him at his castle. Nagelmackers accepted, even though the visit entailed a four-hour detour from the main route. However, the King did not invite them to stay at the castle. They stayed in a hotel and had to walk up a rather steep hill in a downpour to get to the castle. When they left, they got lost and went down a staircase that took them to the back yard, where sentries who thought they were workmen searched them before allowing them to leave.

The run from Ruschuk to Varna was made in four-wheel unbogied carriages over poorly-constructed track. The meals were memorable for partridge so tough it was impossible to chew, and pungent Turkish pastries. The carriages were unheated, but an ample supply of wine and brandy helped the passengers cope with the cold. A small station was robbed and burned by bandits just before the train pulled in. Many passengers got seasick on the Black Sea passage to Constantinople, but in spite of all these discomforts and

traumas, they all returned to Paris on the Orient Express over the same route. The train seemed to be assured of a prosperous future.

The Orient Express was an immediate success, despite the fact that until 1888, the route included the unpleasant Bulgarian stagecoach journey. Finally, in spite of everything the Russians and Bulgarians could to stop it, the line from Constantinople was finished. The first straight-through run from Paris to Constantinople was made in 1888, shaving some 14 hours from the old Varna route.

The train earned a remarkable record of safety and on-time performance although there were a few incidents, the most notable of which was a robbery by Greek bandits in Turkey. They derailed the train and relieved the passengers of their valuables, although the leader returned wedding rings. Some important personages, including some German bankers, were kidnapped and held for ransom. An international crisis seemed imminent until the ransom was paid and the captives released. This so pleased the bandit chief that he gave each of his erstwhile prisoners a gold coin.

In 1929, the train was stranded in a heavy blizzard just inside Turkey for six days before being rescued by Turkish soldiers. The passengers all contributed to buy food from avaricious local peasants. A bomb exploded on a bridge near Budapest in 1931, causing the locomotive and nine cars to fall into a ravine. More than 20 people were killed and hundreds were injured.

Nevertheless, the romance and mystique of the Orient Express developed quickly. Practically

Left: *Wagons-Lits car no. 2419 being taken into Les Invalides, Paris, in 1921. The Armistice ending World War I was signed in it. In 1941 Adolf Hitler had it brought out to provide a revengeful location for the French surrender.*

everybody who was anybody rode on the train at least once, and many of the most important people of the time were regular customers. Transporting royalty was almost a daily occurrence. Leopold II was a frequent rider, traveling to many points attending to his business interests. It seems that he also paid frequent attention to another of his favorite interests – beautiful women – on these excursions. Since he was a large stockholder in Wagons-Lits, he had no trouble arranging accomodations for himself and whatever woman was the love of his life at the moment. It was rumored that the Orient Express was a frequent trysting place for Leopold and one of his favorites, Cleo de Merode, a well-known cabaret singer. This liaision earned him the name Cleopold. He married her a few months before his death and left her a large sum of money. During one of his trips to Constantinople, he managed to bribe his way into a harem while the owner was away. He inadvertently boasted of this feat to the owner, a rather important official in the Ottoman government. An international crisis was avoided when the Turk made no official complaint, apparently because he could not face the prospect of public humiliation.

A prominent prelate of the Russian Orthodox Church traveled on the Orient Express regularly for the sole purpose of spending some time with what were the equivalent of expensive call girls. This kind of transaction was apparently fairly frequent. Conductors made quite a bit of money procuring girls by telegraphing ahead to cooperative stationmasters.

The mysterious munitions tycoon, Sir Basil Zaharoff, was the central figure in one of the most celebrated Orient Express romances. In 1886, when he was 30, he boarded the train in Vienna for a trip to Paris. As usual, he had booked his favorite compartment, no. 7. The train had been delayed because of the late arrival of some important royalty, the 24-year-old Duke of Marchena of the Spanish Bourbons, who was traveling to Paris with his 17-year-old bride Maria. As the story goes, while the train was underway near Salzburg, Zaharoff heard a frantic knocking at his door shortly after 2:00 am. When he opened the door, the young Duchess, clad in a torn peignoir, and with a bloody scratch across her neck, fell into the compartment. She screamed words to the effect that the Duke had gone mad and tried to kill her. In the meantime, the Duke's bodyguard was trying to wrest a dagger away from the incoherent Duke.

The Duke was sent to an asylum and Maria became Zaharoff's mistress. The Spanish royal family was infuriated but there was nothing they could do about it. Zaharoff and Maria had three

In 1931 a bomb exploded on a viaduct near Budapest. The locomotive and nine carriages fell into a ravine, killing more than 20 people.

Below: The opening of the Simplon tunnel between Switzerland and Italy in 1905 provided a more direct route for the Orient Express via Venice and Zagreb. The north portal of the tunnel was opened in 1921.

children. They married when the Duke died, but Maria died two years after the marriage. When Zaharoff died, his bodyguard carried out his last wish. The bodyguard boarded the train in Paris, checking into compartment no. 7 carrying a photograph of Maria that Zaharoff had always kept in his wallet. At exactly 2:32 am, as the train approached Salzburg, the bodyguard tore up the photograph and threw the pieces out the window.

Pieces of photographs were not the only things to be thrown off or fall off the Orient Express. Movies revolving about the Orient Express usually have at least one throwing-off incident (often a spy). Spies are a frequent theme of Orient Express tales, and there were plenty of real spies. It would seem that spies rode the Orient Express for the same reasons anyone else did, which is that until air travel became generally available, it was the fastest, most convenient way to get around in Europe. One spy known to have thrown other spies off the train was Michael Mason, a British intelligence agent assigned to Rumania in the years before World War II. He took on two German spies in the corridor of a Wagons-Lits car, beat them up and threw them off. A World War I era British spy, Sir Robert Baden-Powell, founder of the Boy Scout movement, went about his business disguised as an amateur entomologist taking the Orient Express to collect eastern European butterfly specimens. His sketches of butterflies were actually drawings of fortifications.

One of the better known falling-off incidents involved Paul Deschanel, the President of France. He boarded the train in Paris on 23 May

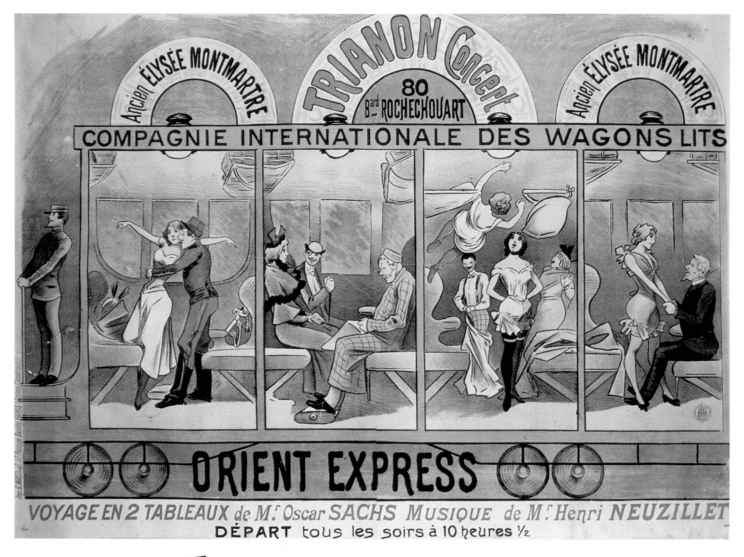

1920, and the next morning he was not to be found. Exactly what happened is still not known. Apparently he opened an exit door, thinking it was a door to a compartment or lavatory, falling off in the process. Remarkably he was not killed or seriously injured, but he was so bruised as to be unrecognizable. Clad in pajamas, he stumbled to the hut of a railway employee, who was not very happy at being awakened and who could not be easily convinced that the apparition standing in his door was the President of the Republic. Of course this was too juicy a story for the press to leave alone. The constant badgering about what really happened was too much for him to bear, and he resigned a few months after the incident.

The Orient Express was not just one train, but a complex collection of feeder lines and alternate routes. One of the most significant events in the train's history occurred in 1906, a year after Nagelmackers' death. In that year, the 12-mile long Simplon Tunnel through the Alps from Switzerland to Italy was completed. The tunnel enabled a route through Milan, Venice, Trieste and Zagreb that proceeded to Constantinople via Belgrade, or a northern route to Bucharest. This was the beginning of the Simplon Orient Express that started officially in 1919, although trains referred to as the Orient Simplon Express traveled that route as soon as the tunnel was opened.

There was no Orient Express service during World War I. Wagons-Lits cars were used for transporting generals and other Allied officials. The war made a museum piece out of Wagons-Lits car no. 2419. The French received the German surrender in that car, and it was retired to the French War Museum at Les Invalides. Adolph Hitler ordered the car removed from the museum in 1940 so he could further humiliate the French

by receiving their surrender in the same car at the same spot that had since been consecrated by the French as a national shrine.

The 1919 agreements for the Simplon Orient Express were worked out at the Versailles Peace Conference as somewhat of a reaction against the recently vanquished Germans. The railways involved were essentially ordered by the negotiators to run trains over specified routes. The idea was to

The Orient Express passes through the Arlberg pass near Innsbruck in Austria.

Bucharest while another went on to Constantinople (which became Istanbul in 1922). This was common practice on the Orient Express lines. Sections of sleeper cars or diners originated in various cities and joined trains at designated points. Vinkovci came to be quite a busy junction town; trains to and from Belgrade, Constantinople, Subotica, Bucharest and Athens exchanged cars here.

Although the victorious Allies wanted to keep Germany from becoming a power again, they did see advantages to running some Wagons-Lits trains through Germany. Accordingly, the Versailles Treaty included a clause specifying that Germany had to supply facilities for running Wagons-Lits trains on their tracks. The Germans managed to delay compliance by pleading poverty, lack of coal, lack of locomotives and so on. A train was not run until June of 1920. The Germans had never been overly cooperative with Wagons-Lits even before the war. In 1916 Germany had formed the Mitropa Gesellschaft, with the intention of breaking the Wagons-Lits monopoly in Austria and Germany, and then in the rest of Europe.

In 1923 French and Belgian troops occupied the Ruhr Valley to punish Germany for not paying war reparations. Germany retaliated by refusing to handle Orient Express trains anywhere in her territory. Not to be stopped by mere Germans, the company worked out a new route running through Basel and Zurich via the Arlberg Tunnel into Austria. The resulting Arlberg Orient Express turned out to be a very popular train, reaping handsome profits from transporting businessmen to important cities in Central and Eastern Europe in just a few hours.

When the French and Belgians withdrew from the Ruhr, Germany immediately offered to accomodate Wagons-Lits trains again, but the Simplon and Arlberg routes were so successful, the Company was in no hurry. For a while they only ran the train three days a week through Germany. Germany continued to build up Mitropa, and when the Nazis came to power, Hitler deliberately harrassed Wagons-Lits trains with 'track repairs' and similar tactics.

From 1924 on, the company stopped making wooden cars and began to construct steel cars. These cars were painted a rich blue with gold trim, giving them a distinctive look that immediately identified them as Wagons-Lits. Speed began to increase as more lines over which Orient Express trains ran became electrified. Speeds of 75 miles an hour were attained on short stretches by the 1930s.

The period between the two world wars is regarded by many railway historians as the age of luxury. In 1926 the Simplon Orient Express service was extended to Cairo. This luxurious service, called the Taurus Express on the leg from Istanbul to Cairo, involved ferry crossings at the Bosporus and the Suez Canal. Wagons-Lits supplied extraordinarily opulent Pullman cars for the run from the Suez Canal to Cairo. Luxury or not,

link the victorious allies – Great Britain, France and Italy with Rumania and the newly established kingdom of Yugoslavia, without having to pass through German, Hungarian or Austrian territory. For the convenience of British passengers, the service started at Calais.

The train followed the Milan-Venice-Trieste route to Zagreb and beyond. At the Yugoslav town of Vinkovci, one section split off for

Right: *The table setting specially designed and produced for the recreated Venice Simplon Orient Express which made its inaugural run from Victoria Station, London in May 1982.*
Opposite top: *The lavatory floor of the Pullman car Cygnus is a mosaic depicting the legend of Leda and the swan.*
Opposite center: *Car No 3544 has a large washroom. It formed part of the Dutch Royal Train from 1946 to 1948.*

Below: *The refurbished interior of the dining car Zena, built in 1928.*

Top: A poster of Victoria Station by Fix-Masseau. Above: A poster of Milan Station by the same artist. Left: A sleeping compartment in car No 3543 in its night-time configuration.

the passengers had to contend with a transfer to a bus from Tripoli, Syria (now Lebanon) to Haifa.

The golden jubilee year of the Wagons-Lits Company, which came in 1926, was marked by the launching of the Fleche d'Or or Golden Arrow, from London to Paris via Calais, a service that linked the British Pullman network with Wagons-Lits operations on the continent. Although various political and financial squabbles kept it from being officially called the Fleche d'Or until 1929, everybody called it that from the outset. Golden Arrow passengers were put on a special boat train that got them to Dover later than anyone else. They could also have the best choice of seats on the ferry. Baggage was put in sealed containers in London so passengers wouldn't be bothered with customs searches until they got to Paris. Luxury passengers were saved the bother of leaving their sleepers to get on the ferry when the 'Night Ferry' was started in 1936. This ferry took the cars across the channel from England to France.

Other European luxury trains of the period included the Côte d'Azur Pullman, Edelweiss, Rheingold, and Sud Express. The Cote d'Azur ran from Paris to the Mediterranean via Lyon. The interiors of the Cote d'Azur cars were probably among the best examples of the *Art Nouveau* of the period. The Rheingold was Mitropa's bid for scenery-loving tourists. The route chosen for this Holland to Swiss Alps service ran through the spectacularly beautiful Rhine gorge between Cologne and Mainz.

In the United States, the inter-wars period saw the start of luxury trains such as the Super Chief and the Hiawathas.

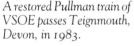

A restored Pullman train of VSOE passes Teignmouth, Devon, in 1983.

In 1932 the Orient Express service to Istanbul (the former Constantinople) via Stuttgart and Vienna was restored. In spite of the economic depression, Wagons-Lits continued to thrive. Airlines were not yet competitive, and automobile travel was slow. When Germany annexed Austria in 1938, all contracts with Wagons-Lits for local services were broken, and the German Mitropa Company took over. In spite of pressure from Hitler, Mussolini continued to allow the Simplon Orient Express to operate in northern Italy after the war started in 1939. The 'phony war' became a real one with the blitzkrieg of 1940, and wherever the Germans advanced, it was the intention that Mitropa should take over.

Hundreds of Wagons-Lits cars were stranded in various parts of Europe during the war. Many of these were destroyed in military actions, broken up for scrap and used by Germans for various purposes such as troop transport and temporary barracks. Very few were recovered. Hitler ran an erstatz Orient Express that was used mainly by high ranking SS and Army officers.

That most famous Wagons-Lits car of all, no. 2419, was taken to Berlin and put on public display. As the war began to close in on Germany, Hitler had the car removed from Berlin and destroyed, not wanting it to once again fall into the hands of the Allies.

After the war's end the Orient Express started again, and soon faced new problems imposed by the 'Iron Curtain' and the growing East-West conflict. More spies than ever before became regular customers, and the number of 'accidents' involving passengers increased accordingly. Many an official of a Communist country got a little taste of western decadent luxury on the Orient Express.

In 1950 a beautiful Hungarian girl who happened to be the mistress of the Hungarian Head of State tried to seduce a CIA agent. Several weeks later, the mangled body of the CIA agent was

found in a tunnel near Salzburg. The Austrian Police obtained a confession from some Rumanians several months after the incident. The Rumanians said they killed him and threw him off on orders from a 'foreign government.'

Intrigue and foul deeds on the Orient Express became a favorite theme of writers. Probably the best known work of fiction on the Orient Express is Agatha Christie's *Murder on the Orient Express*. Agatha Christie knew the Orient Express well. She frequently accompanied her first husband, a British intelligence agent, on trips to the Middle East. This experience enabled her to provide an impeccably accurate background for her Belgian detective, Hercule Poirot, as he went about catching the murderer with his 'little grey cells.' In the lavish 1974 film based on the book, the train is as much the star as Peter Ustinov, Vanessa Redgrave, Ingrid Bergman, Sir John Gielgud, or any of the others in the illustrious cast. An Orient Express was also the locale for Alfred Hitchcock's *The Lady Vanishes*. James Bond's Agent 007 perpetrated his own brand of romance and mayhem on the Orient Express in *From Russia with Love*. Graham Greene's 1932 detective novel, *Stamboul Train* was another Orient Express yarn.

As a new generation of pleasure travelers and businessmen forsook trains for airplanes and automobiles in the 1960s and 1970s, hard times fell on the Orient Express. The old Orient Express did not die swiftly and painlessly. Starting in 1961, there was a series of 'farewell' runs. It limped along into the 1970s in various guises, all of which were pathetic shadows of what the Orient Express had been. In the final years, complete runs to Istanbul were rare, and it became difficult to identify any particular set of cars running over the route at a given time as *the* Orient Express. Cars starting out from Paris would be shunted to different destinations at various points. Cars of various classes and descriptions, including freight wagons and cattle cars, would be added here and there. Border crossings into Iron Curtain countries were sometimes harrowing experiences, involving delays of several hours. Occasionally, passengers would be forced to wait outside the train on freezing winter nights.

The regular through sleeping cars between Paris and Istanbul via the Direct Orient and Marmara expresses ceased in May 1977. As expected, most of the passengers on this final run were enthusiasts, but they found none of the old glories on what turned out to be a rather inglorious final run. The train was late leaving, and there were no luxurious diners. No meal service was provided and only one sleeper was included. Passengers had to carry their own food supply. This final Marmara Express which carried the through car from Paris pulled into Istanbul about five hours late. Just how final this 'final' run was depends on one's definition of the word. Trains continued to go to Istanbul and travel agents continued to offer various 'Orient Express tours.'

Today's Orient Express, began with a Sother-

by's auction in Monte Carlo in October 1977. Five classic Wagons-Lits cars which had been used in the film "Murder on the Orient-Express" were bought by James Sherwood, President of SeaCo Inc., and Sea Containers Ltd. Sherwood assembled some 27 Pullman and Wagons-Lits cars, which were meticulously rebuilt to become the fleet of the restored Venice Simplon Orient Express. The first new VSOE left Paris bound for Venice, on 25 May 1984.

By 1984, the new VSOE was running three times a week from London to Venice. The new service has been a great success.

Top: *Fine food and chateaux-bottled wine are among one of the many attractions of travel on the Venice Simplon Orient Express. Seen here is the dining car Cygnus, en route between London and Folkestone.*
Above: *A publicity photograph shows restored Car No 3644 Cygnus. It was built in 1929 in France.*

Supertrains of Europe

Most of today's luxurious, high speed trains are in Europe. There are many reasons for this concentration of railway superlatives there. Railways have been in operation on that continent longer than in the rest of the world, and much of the expertise in railway technology is there. As mentioned earlier, distances between major European cities are shorter than in the United States, a situation that tends to dull the competitive edge of air travel's greater speed. However, much of the incentive to make the investments in money and technological know-how that made super trains a reality came from the foresight of a man named FQ den Hollander.

Den Hollander was the president of Netherlands Railways in the 1950s. He warned his fellow railway executives that unless some extraordinary measures were taken, European railways would lose out to the growing airlines and the automobile.

The resurgent post-war economy created a need for fast, dependable business travel, particularly for one-day trips in which the traveler reached his destination in time for a full day's work and could return to his home city in time for dinner. In the immediate post-war period, European railways were grievously ill-equipped to provide this kind of service. Most international trains carried mail as well as passengers, necessitating many stops. Then there were the border checks which could go on for hours. And if the customs officials and border guards were, by some strange alteration of mood, fast and courteous on a particular day, the inevitable changing of locomotives and crews could well take a few hours longer than usual to make up for the time gained. Airplanes had a decided advantage in that they could not stop in mid-air at borders no matter how officious the functionaries on the ground. Of course, the passengers had to go through the border check routine once they got to the airport. But if the aircraft had flown over three countries, the passengers would have to endure only one customs check compared to three for the hapless passengers making the same trip by train.

Den Hollander made a rather sweeping proposal to the transport ministers of France, Luxembourg, West Germany, the Netherlands, Switzerland and Italy. He proposed the formation of an international network of deluxe trains between the main commercial centers of western Europe to be called Trans-Europ Express (TEE). TEE was to be run by an international body funded by the participating nations, but it would not be under their adminstrative control or subject to any financial restrictions imposed by any country. He wanted TEE train sets to be of a standard design

The Glacier Express on the Furka Oberalp Railway in Switzerland.

The TEE Cisalpin express leaves Brig, Switzerland, en route from Milan to Paris via the Simplon tunnel.

Above: *A TEE trainset of French National Railways (SNCF).*

Opposite: *The Swiss Express leaving St Gallen for Geneva hauled by an Re 4/4 III locomotive. A local train is behind it.*

that offered luxurious, fast service. Customs checks would be done while the train was underway, and the trains would be first class only with no local stops, mail or other encumberances.

While the participating countries embraced den Hollander's idea in principle, they did so with reservations based on national interest. The TEE that emerged was rife with many technological, political and economic problems, but it did provide the kind of service that was needed for the railways to compete, and the concept encouraged many railways to provide improved trains, many of which properly deserve to be called super trains.

The nations involved agreed on a number of things including an exclusive first-class market, supplementary fare, trains capable of at least 87 mph, seats no more than three to a side, dining cars and border formalities while on the move. They even agreed on the colors for the trains – red and cream, with the shades precisely specified and supplied to all participating railways by the same paint factory in Switzerland. That, however, is where the agreement stopped and the quibbling began.

While they were harmonious on the color scheme, they could not agree on a standard train set. As might be expected, they could not agree to an independent governing body. While the governments involved gave lip service to the idea of faster border checks, TEE trains were still stopped at borders, but the checks tended to be perfunctory. The TEE that emerged was a rather loose association of seven railways, each of which acted as overall manager in rotation for terms of four years. Each railway kept whatever revenue it generated, and contributed whatever equipment it chose to the TEE fleet, restricted only by the broad specifications of the agreement. All of this was a big disappointment to den Hollander, but if

one considers that it happened less than 10 years after the war, and before the establishment of the European Common Market, it was quite a remarkable achievement.

France's contribution was its RGP diesel train set that had been more or less standard on French domestic service since 1954. There was really nothing wrong with this equipment, but contributions such as these dimmed the few lingering hopes of standardization, and before long there was little distinction between TEE trains and the regular inter-city services run in each country.

Double-ended diesel trainsets were chosen for early TEE service for a number of reasons. First of all, electrification between the various cities was not complete. Even if electrification had been complete, four different current supply systems were in use in the seven participating countries – 25,000 V DC in most of France, 15,000 V AC in Germany, Austria and Switzerland, 3000 V DC in Belgium and Italy and 1500 V DC in the Netherlands and parts of France. Locomotives that could change from one system to another were not yet available. Consequently, there was a great deal of wasteful running of diesel trains on electrified track. Finally, some of the stations were terminals where the turnaround of locomotive-hauled trains was a time-consuming affair.

The German contribution to TEE was the last diesel trainset built in Germany for long-distance work. These trains were among the best in use on TEE routes, offering better comfort at higher speeds than other diesel trainsets at the time.

By 1958, the Swiss had four-voltage electric train sets available for use in the TEE system. These trains made it possible for transalpine routes to be included in TEE offerings. Diesels had not been particularly satisfactory for the pull over the Alps. These train sets started service in 1961 as the Cisalpin running from Milan to Paris

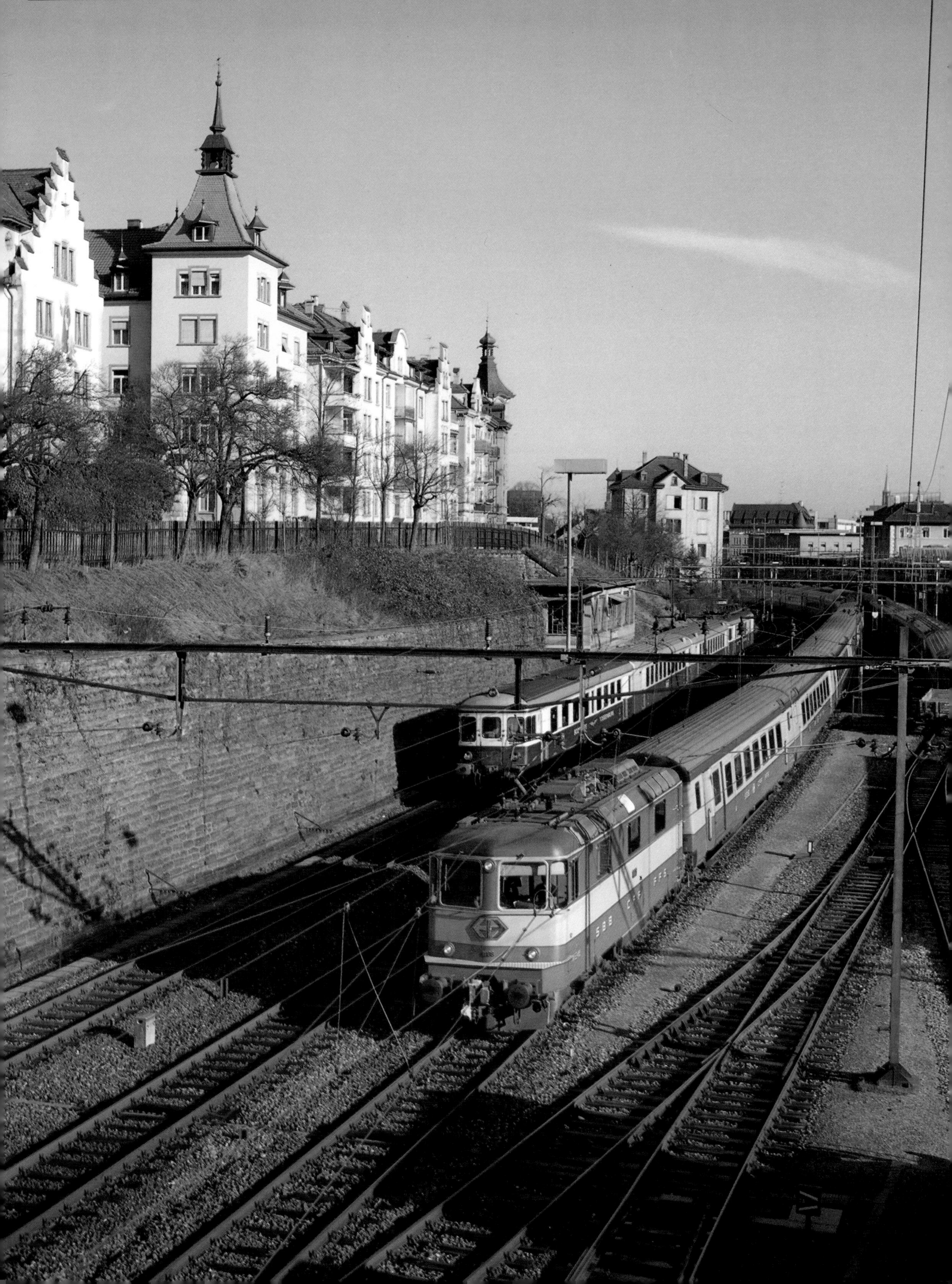

via the Simplon Tunnel, and the Gottard and Ticino service to Milan, Zurich and Basel via the Gotthard Tunnel.

Electrification continued in the rest of western Europe at a rapid pace, making it possible to upgrade other trains. The Rheingold Express in 1962 became a first-class-only train with air-conditioning, observation domes, bar cars, observation lounges and more. It set a new standard for luxury train service. Unlike previous TEE trains, the Rheingold was not a trainset. It was and still is pulled by an electric locomotive. The class 103.1 locomotives now used on the Rheingold and other fast German inter-city trains is capable of 125 mph. Special high-geared versions have reached 155 mph. The adoption of locomotives for the Rheingold and other TEE trains, particularly those on the heavily traveled Paris-Brussels-Amsterdam route, marked a temporary decline of the trainset for high-speed runs in Europe. Early trainsets did not give as comfortable a ride as locomotive-hauled trains. The trainset was far from finished. The Japanese demonstrated the speed capabilities of the electric train set in 1964 with the 130 mph Shinkansen or bullet trains. From the mid-1970s a new generation of electric train sets became the fastest trains in the world.

The concept of TEE as an international operation became somewhat blurred with the designa-

tion of France's Mistral as TEE in 1965. The Mistral, which runs from Paris south to the Riviera, is a fast, luxurious train, but it is not international.

Spain's Talgo trains were accorded TEE status in 1969, which was rather remarkable since the Spanish Railways gauge is 5 feet 6 inches while the rest of the railways in western Europe employ a 4 foot 8½ inch gauge. These trains could not join the system until the perfection of a variable-gauge axle that enables the gauge to be changed at the Franco-Spanish border. The Talgo is an unusual train designed to overcome some of the conditions of Spanish railways that tend to limit speed. The cars have a low center of gravity. Each car has only one axle at one end. The end without an axle is articulated with the axled end of the car in front of it. This arrangement results in a rather flexible train that can negotiate curves on flaky roadbeds faster than can conventional trains. The TEE Talgo is called the Catalan Talgo and it runs from Barcelona to Geneva.

Many of today's European supertrains were originally TEE trains, while others had nothing to do with that organization. However, there can be little doubt that without den Hollander's pioneering efforts there would be fewer trains in the world, let alone Europe, worthy of being called super trains. Following is a closer look at some of today's European supertrains.

A type ETR401 of Italian State Railways. The Pendolino has a positive tilt mechanism which allows corners to be taken at high speeds.

ITALY

The ETR 300 Settebello seven-car train set is not the fastest train in Europe or even in Italy, but it is one of most luxurious trains in the world, and it has a special place in the history of European railways. The Settebello is an electric train, powered by a 3000 V direct current, overhead wire system. Its origins go back to 1939, when Mussolini was determined to show the world that Italian railways were just as good if not better than those of any other country. And he did just that, at least as far as speed was concerned.

The train that was chosen to demonstrate Italy's railway progress to the world was a three-car high-speed electric set designated Class ETR 200. On 20 July 1939 it set out on a 196-mile trip from Milan to Rome via the newly completed 11.5 mile Appenine Tunnel. For this demonstration run, the line voltage had been increased from 3000 to 4000 V. The run was made in one hour and 55 minutes for an average speed of 102 mph. The top speed reached was 126 mph, a record that was to stand until 1964 when it was surpassed by a Japanese Shinkansen train. Il Duce made his point, but he and everybody who was on the train were lucky it stayed on the tracks, which was in no condition for such high speed runs.

Today's Settebello is a lavishly luxurious train with an appearance that truly merits the description of unique. At each end of the train there is a rounded-off observation lounge skirted by what appear to be balloon fenders lifted from a 1930s luxury sedan. The driver or engineer sits in a kind of enclosed crow's nest on top of the observation car. This arrangement has resulted in a very roomy and open observation car. Sitting in the front observation car as the train curves it way through the Appenines between Florence and Bologna is an unforgettable, and to some, an unnerving experience. The Settebello's electric braking system is so efficient that the engineer does not have to start braking until the train is practically on top of the curve. The seeming imminence of flying off the side of the mountain has been compared to the feeling of riding a roller coaster.

The internal appointments of the Settebello are exceptionally luxurious. Service in the dining car is *table d'hote*. Diner furniture is polished wood, and there are murals on the walls. There is a fully equipped bar, and the lounges are furnished with settees and free-standing arm chairs.

The train has ten bogies, six of which are powered with a pair of 1500 V motors. Because of track conditions, today's Settebellos do not run at the speeds set in the 1939 demonstration run. Nevertheless, the speeds are still respectable. The Settebello set is capable of running at 125 mph. However, new lines under construction will theoretically allow speeds of 156 mph. A section of the Rome-Milan line opened in 1977 allowed speeds of 112 mph on some parts of the run.

It is not too difficult to build a locomotive or trainset that will go as fast as you want it to go. All you have to do is supply it with enough power.

The hard part is designing the components so they will have sufficient stability at high speeds to give a comfortable ride, keep the pantographs or other power pick-up devices in contact with the power source, and, most importantly, keep the train on the tracks, particularly on curves. There are two basic approaches to the problem. One is to build a high-precision roadbed with tolerances measured in fractions of millimeters, meticulously canted tracks, and no short-radius curves. As

Top: *An electric express train on the Rome-Florence line.*
Above: *The first-class dining car on a TEE express in Italy. An enjoyable meal!*

The Settobello of Italian State Railways running from Rome to Florence.

one might expect, that is a very expensive alternative. The other is build the train so that it tilts as it goes around a canted curve. That is a far less expensive choice than special roadbeds, but as many railway executives have discovered to their sorrow, it is not the most dependable option.

The ETR 401 Pendolino four-car train is a handsome trainset with a body-tilting mechanism. Powered by a 3000 V catenary system, the train is capable of speeds of 156 mph – *if* the tilt mechanism works properly. Italy was the first European country (Japan was first in the world) to get a tilting train into regular service. The tilting mechanism allows a maximum tilt of 9° and is positively actuated, as opposed to passive systems which tilt in response to physical forces as the train rounds the curve. The Pendolino's tilt system is controlled by gyroscopes and accelerometers.

The Pendolino went into service on the trans-Appenine route between Rome and Ancona. It is able to get up to full speed on only a short portion of this 185 mile route. The tilting mechanism comes into full use on the winding curves of the mountain line. The Fiat-built train has an electromagnetic rail brake in addition to pneumatic air brakes used at slow speeds, and an electric braking system for use at high speeds. The latter turns the motors into generators.

WEST GERMANY

The West Germans were the pioneers of the 125 mph plus train in Europe, but they were careful pioneers. Left with what was essentially half a system – and a rather disrupted and disorganized one – when Germany was divided after World War II, the Germans had some massive rebuilding to do before they could think about high-speed trains. Starting in the 1960s, Deutsche Bundesbahn (DB), the West German Railways, began a program of line improvements for the purpose of running 125 mph inter-city trains. Track between Munich and Augsburg and Hanover and Celle was fitted with new automatic speed control and cab signalling systems.

Attempts to extend speeds to 150 mph and beyond began with the construction of Neubaustrecken, starting in the 1970s. These are bypasses around sections of track that presently restrict speed. However, progress on the Neubaustrecken has been slow. In the mid 1980s, the top speed of West Germany's inter-city trains were still 125 mph.

The post-war Rheingold began in 1951 as an ordinary train. It continued that way until electrification of all its old route from the mouth of the Rhine to the Alps was completed. The completion was the impetus needed for the DB to restore in 1962 the Rheingold to its pre-war status as a luxurious, high-speed train. The cars were all air-conditioned, a feature still unusual enough in the Europe of the early 1960s to generate attention. To the casual observer, the most obvious innovations were the vista-domed observation

Above: A Class 103 locomotive of German State Railways hauls the Munich-Amsterdam Senator express along the Rhine valley.
Left: Germany's high speed train, the ET403 provides a rail/air link between Dusseldorf and Frankfurt airport.

cars. DB hoped to attract the scenery-lover market with these cars that looked somewhat like greenhouses on wheels. These cars have since been discontinued. The suspensions of the cars gave an exceptionally smooth ride and there were telephones on board as well as secretarial service to cater to the needs of the business traveler DB hoped to attract.

Real speed came with the development of the Class 103.1 electric locomotive. Specifications were drawn up in 1961 for an electric locomotive that could maintain a speed of 125 mph. Acceleration to top speed was to be in no more than 150 seconds. Four prototypes were delivered in 1963 and they stole the show at the Munich Internationl Transport Exhibition of that year. The 103.1's first job was hauling a special train from Munich to Augsburg which it did at an average speed of 88 mph, reaching 125 mph at several points.

From 1970 on, some 145 of these powerful machines were built, many of which incorporated

Above (both): *The vistadome on the* Rheingold *express of German State Railways. This has now been discontinued – it used to get rather hot in the summer. When in operation it provided splendid views, especially of the lower Rhine valley.*

Right: *The* Rheingold *diner car provides meals ranging from light snacks to full dinner.*

improvements that enabled the locomotive to pull heavier loads at its rated speed. The full potential of the 103.1 was realized with the formation of the German inter-city network, IC-Zuge. The addition of second class coaches to many of the fast trains in the system meant that the 103.1 would have to haul longer trains. A specially modified version, 103.118, has a top speed of 155 mph. As of this writing it was undergoing high-speed tests. It is the most powerful single-unit locomotive in the world. Other luxury trains pulled by the 103.1 include the Blauer Enzian (Hamburg-Munich) and Helvetia (Hamburg-Zurich).

The successful and economic running of some of the TEE trainsets encouraged DB to build its own high-speed trainset, the ET 403. This is a 125 mph trainset with power supplied to all axles. The streamlined, beak-like rake of the cab soon had people calling these trains Donald Ducks. On-board transformers and thyristors convert the 15,000 V 16 2/3 cycle alternating current supplied from overhead wires to direct current. The trucks or bogies incorporate an air suspension system that also serves as a body tilting system. The train body can be tilted as much as 4° on curves by varying the pressure in the air bags that provide the suspension.

ET 403 trains were first used in public service on the Munich-Bremen route, which at 485 miles is one of the longest domestic rail services in West

Germany. The decision to include second-class coaches on high-speed inter-city trains marked the end of further expansion of ET 403 service. Trainsets do not have the flexibility of locomotive-hauled trains which allowed for the adding of cars as needed. However, one can still ride an ET 403. In 1982, Lufthansa, the German state airline, initiated high speed connecting service from the Frankfurt Airport to Cologne, Bonn and Düsseldorf. The trains running on this high-speed service are ET 403s.

Top: An early German TEE diesel locomotive. Above: A German VT 10 501 streamlined diesel locomotive dating from 1948.

Main picture: *The glory of British steam locomotives preserved. The LNER class A3 Pacific No 4472* Flying Scotsman *heads north from Newark on its Diamond Jubilee run in March 1983.*
Inset below: *The Golden Arrow provided a service from London to the port of Dover and the Channel ferries to France. It is shown here at its commencement in 1951.*
Inset bottom: *The LNER A4 Pacific No 4488* Sir Nigel Gresley. *The A4's, designed by Gresley, were among the finest steam locomotives ever built. One of them, Mallard, holds the world steam speed record of 126 mph.*

GREAT BRITAIN

As might be expected, the British railway system was not in particularly good shape at the end of World War II. The problems were not so much from German bombs as from the lines pushing themselves to beyond the limit to keep up with the war effort. Between the two World Wars, one could ride on some very fine, fast luxury trains in Britain. Precursors of the Flying Scotsman, for example, had been leaving Kings Cross in London at 10:00 every morning since 1862. The name, Flying Scotsman, came about during the speed wars of the 1880s between the West Coast and the East Coast lines. The Flying Scotsman cut the London-Edinburgh time from 9 hours to 7 hours and 15 minutes. The speed war might have gone on forever, but the companies voluntarily agreed to restrict the London-Edinburgh time to 8 hours and 15 minutes in reaction to stories of frightening, swaying rides, during which the trains shook and bounced so fiercely they seemed to stay on the tracks only through divine intervention. This 'gentlemen's agreement' remained until 1932.

In the years between the wars, British travelers both first and third class came to expect a high level of service on trains such as The Flying Scotsman, the Royal Scot, the Queen of Scots, and (for first class passengers only) on the Golden Arrow. After World War I, there was agitation to nationalize the railways, as had been done in most countries on the continent. However, the British did not go the whole way to nationalization at this time, opting instead, in 1923, to reorganize the various lines into four large companies: the London, Midland and Scottish (LMS), London and

North Eastern (LNER), Great Western (GWR), Southern (SR). The Flying Scotsman was the premier offering of the LNER. By 1930 it had such amenities as a beauty salon and a ladies' retiring room. In the late 1930s it was hauled by the famous streamlined steam engine, the Gresley A4 Pacific. However, the Flying Scotsman was not the first train to be hauled by this class of locomotive. That honor went to the Silver Jubilee in 1935. On the inaugural run, speeds were well over 100 mph, reaching 112.5 mph maximum.

When a Socialist government was elected in 1945, nationalization of the railways in Britain seemed inevitable. British Railways, the state railway of Britain, came into existence in 1948. There was, of course, no immediate return to the luxury pre-war standards, but British Railways did make an effort with a variety of Pullman services. While British Railways were not part of the TEE network, the management was sufficiently impressed with TEE operations to go after the luxury market with Pullman trainsets. The best known of the British Railways Pullman sets were the Blue Pullmans. These trains had a reasonable supply of luxury appointments and their ride was good.

Plans for modernization drawn up in the 1950s included provisions for electricifcation, but electrifiction of lines went much more slowly in Britain than on the continent. British Railway management were as aware of the looming competition from air and road as anyone else, and they also knew that increased speeds were vital if they were to compete. Accordingly they began look for a way to achieve, or at least approach, electrification speeds without electrification. They found it in the Class 55 Deltic diesel-elecric locomotive, one of the finest, if not the very finest, high-speed passenger diesels ever built.

The double-ended, snub-nosed Deltics were equipped with two 18-cylinder 1750 hp two-stroke diesel engines. The name Deltic came from the layout of the engines which could be briefly described as an inverted Greek letter delta ($\triangle$). Three banks of double cylinders, each with a pair of opposed pistons, were arranged so that they formed the three sides of the delta. The banks of pistons were connected to the crankshaft at the points of the delta. This arrangement achieved one of the most advantageous weight/power ratios ever managed with a diesel-6.2 lb per horsepower. This was about 250% better than other diesel locomotives in use at the time.

A prototype was available in 1955, and subsequent testing revealed the Deltic to be a fast and remarkably dependable machine. Its maximum speed was rated at 100 mph, and when it went into regular service in 1961 it pulled heavy passenger trains up 5% grades at speeds between 90 and 100 mph. British Railways found itself with the most powerful single-unit diesel locomotive in the world. In keeping with a tradition of the old LNER, each Deltic was named after a winning race horse or Scottish and English regiments.

Deltics were put into service hauling trains such as the Flying Scotsman. They cut the London-Edinburgh time to 5 hours and 30 minutes. British Railways soon began to enjoy healthy increases in passenger traffic and revenues. The last Deltic-hauled train pulled into King's Cross on 2 January 1982.

The 1968 Transport Act of Parliament resulted in sweeping reorganizations and cuts of service. The main victims were the small branch lines which could not compete with automobiles, buses and trucks. All that remain of these are a few museum lines run by railway enthusiasts. However, the act also provided for government subsidies to keep passenger service going on main lines and some branches.

A British Rail Deltic diesel locomotive pulls the Flying Scotsman *over Welwyn Viaduct in 1962.*

The next step was the development of British Railway's Inter-City service – 125 mph trains aggressively marketed to lure passengers away from airlines and out of their Austins, Rovers and Jaguars. The first of these trains was the HST 125, which is still one of the most super of super trains.

The name of this train is self-descriptive. HST stands for high speed train, and the 125 is for 125 mph. What the name does not tell you is that it is one of the great success stories of modern railroading. The HST is a diesel-electric high speed train. This is a double-ended train: that is, power units are located at each end. Each power unit is equipped with a lightweight V-12 diesel engine rated at 2250 hp. The engines turn integral alternators which feed current to four motors mounted in the bogie frames.

The basic idea of the HST was to provide superfast service without having to embark on expensive alterations of existing lines. The major ingredient in the success of the concept was keeping the trains as technologically conservative as possible. Most of the technology employed in the HST 125 was an update of previous proven concepts, instead of completely new innovations. Entirely new technology often looks fine on the drawing boards only to fail in actual use. Since the power units of the HST 125 were intended only for use in this train, they could be built simply.

Prototypes were tested in the early 1970s. On one of these tests, a prototype HST 125 reached 143 mph, a record that still stands for diesel traction. The HST 125 went into regular public service in October of 1976 on the main line from London's Paddington Station to Bristol and South Wales. It immediately set average speeds of 90 to 101 mph, exceeded at the time only by Japan's Shinkansen trains. Placed on the Flying Scotsman route, the HST 125 reduced the time between London and Edinburgh to 4 hours and 37

minutes, shaving almost an hour from the Deltic's 5½ hours on the 392.8 mile route.

Redesign of the coaches resulted in a degree of comfort never before attained with a trainset. Sophisticated bogies utilizing air suspension systems help to smooth the ride, and efficient sound-proofing and air-conditioning also add to passenger comfort.

The APT was intended to be the next generation of high-speed British Railway trains after the HST 125. The development of the APT (APT stands for advanced passenger train) was one of the most ambitious engineering projects ever attempted. Sadly, as is often the case with trail-blazing technology, the project has been plagued with many problems, all of which are minor, but have been enough to keep the train out of service for extended periods.

In its present configuration, the APT is an electric high-speed passenger train. It runs on a 25,000 V 50 cycle overhead wire system. An on-board step-down transformer and thyristor-based control system feeds current to four 1000 hp

Top: *The Midland Pullman on trial in 1960.* Above: *British Rail's hope for the future, the Advanced Passenger Train (APT). Despite heavy investment the computerized tilting mechanism has yet to prove itself.*

motors mounted in the bodies of the power cars in
the center of the train.

Basic research on the APT began in the 1960s.
The idea was to design a train to run at speeds of
150 mph on existing track, some of which was
sharply curved. The basis of this ability was to be a
body-tilting system similar to those used on trains
in Italy, Japan and Canada. A controlled tilting
system, rather than a passive one, was the design
goal.

The tilting system that was built was equipped
with electronic sensors that respond to the movement of the coach ahead. The cars can tilt as
much as 9°. When the train is at maximum tilt,
one side of the car can be some 16 inches higher
than the other. The profile of the cars is such that
at maximum tilt they are unable to make contact

with a train on the adjoining track.

Other innovations include a highly sophisticated suspension system and a mechanism in the
bogies that allows self-steering. The braking system was also innovative. A hydrokinetic or water
turbine brake was developed for the APT which
enables it to stop in as little as 2000 yards from full
speed. A more conventional disc-brake system is
used to stop and slow the train at lower speeds.

The prototype, tested in 1973, was fitted with a
gas turbine engine. In tests, this version attained
a speed of 151 mph. However, British Railways
decided to go for electric propulsion. Following
the 1973 Middle East Wars, the price of oil
soared, making a turbine far too expensive to run.
No diesel engine with a suitable power/weight
ratio was available, and some of the most heavily-
traveled, potentially lucrative routes were now
elecrified. Notable among these were lines from
London to Liverpool, Glasgow and Manchester.

The first APT trains with electric power were
ready in 1978, but scores of little problems kept it
from going into service. However, some of these
minor defects resulted in potential disasters.
There was a derailment at 100 mph, for example.
On the inaugural run in December 1981 there
were three emergency stops caused by a malfunc-
tion in the body-tilting system. Tilt mechanism
malfunctions activate a system that locks the cars
upright and automatically pulls the emergency
stop cord. Pots, pans and other assorted equipment were scattered in the dining car galley, and
a few passengers were shaken up. The cause of all
this havoc was believed to be a blown fuse. The
train was taken out of service, and its future still
remains uncertain, although it has been running
satisfactorily in public service recently.

FRANCE

SNCF's post-World War II plans centered about rapid electrification with the intended purpose of establishing fast, frequent inter-city service aimed at the first-class business market. The high-speed tests with the CC 7100 and BB 9004 electric locomotives discussed earlier were an important part of SNCF's development plans. Among the best known of these trains was the Mistral (Paris-Lyon-Marseilles-Nice) and the Aquitaine (Paris-Bordeaux). These trains were among the most luxurious trains to run in Europe since the Orient Express. They were furnished with bars and diners, of course. In addition, they had shops, boutiques, telephones and other conveniences.

Two of the finest electric locomotives in the world were built to haul these trains and other French and TEE service, the Class 40100 and the Class 15000.

The Class 40100 locomotives were among the first designed to operate on all four of the voltages and frequencies used on participating TEE lines. Introduced in the mid 1960s, these machines have a top speed of 112 mph. These are handsome machines with rakish Z-shaped ends, and a red stripe running down the silvery sides, all of which

SNCF adopted a different approach to the challenge of high speed rail travel and constructed new lines for their gas-turbine Train à Grande Vitesse (TGV). The line was built to avoid sharp curves and thus to allow high speeds. Seen here is the prototype 001.

Above: *The TEE trainset Parsifal arrives at Paris-Nord from Dortmund in 1958, hauled by an RGP diesel.*

Right: *A Belgian 1800 class multi-voltage CC approaches Welkenaedt with the 13.53 Ostend-Cologne express in 1983.*

seem to evoke speed. Designed by the French industrial artist Paul Arzens, the rake of the cab is for more than just show. The steep incline of the front window was intended to reduce sun glare in the engineer's cab.

Rectifiers and transformers change the overhead current to 1500 V which is fed to two 2190 hp motors mounted on the bogies. Divided armature windings allow combinations of parallel and series circuits, depending on which country's current is being used. A flexible drive system provides gearing of the motors to all of the three axles.

The Class 15000 is a dual-voltage locomotive designed to be run on the two voltages used on French railways. The idea was to eliminate the time-consuming changing of locomotives. With a maximum speed of 112 mph, the 15000 has two 2960 hp motors, one mounted on each bogie.

Regular service began in the mid 1970s, and they soon earned a reputation for speed and dependability. A similar locomotive, Class 72000, was run for long distances at 125 mph in the late 1970s. The number designations on these locomotives are based on voltage combinations.

The culmination of French efforts to provide the best high-speed luxury service is the magnificent *Train à Grande Vitesse*, the state of the art in rail travel today.

The evolution of the TGV was a logical series of events. By 1960, traffic on the line connecting Paris, Lyon and Marseilles, the three largest cities

in France, was so congested that track time had to be essentially rationed between passenger trains and slower freight service. French railway technology had advanced to the point where speed in excess of 150 mph was possible, but not feasible because of the state of tracks and signalling. The obvious solution was to build a new line, and as long as you had to build a new line why not build it to accomodate the high speeds that were now possible? It was immediately apparent that trains running on the new line at speeds in excess of 150 mph and even 160 mph would be formidable competition indeed for air and highway travel.

Initial studies began in the mid-1960s. One of the first and most important decisions was to limit the new line to passenger traffic. Track designers could then concentrate on the needs of high-speed passenger trains. Following the record-breaking trails of the CC7100 and the BB9004 in 1955, SNCF continued its investigations into high speeds. Some regular service speeds of 124 mph were allowed on short stretches of the Paris-Bordeaux line. An experimental gas turbine train set was run at 147 mph, and production sets reached speeds of 155 mph.

The first trains designated TGV were experimental gas turbines which reached speeds of 197 mph. These runs were indeed impressive and they served to convince SNCF executives that the fast trains running on the new Paris-Lyon line would be these gas turbines. However, as was the case with the APT, the oil crisis of 1973 made gas

Above: *The TGV at Dijon. Although lines have been specially constructed for the high speed trains, they also form part of the national network.*

Right: *Gas-turbine motive power is also used on ordinary main lines. RTG trains, pictured here, stand at the Gare St Lazare ready for runs to Cherbourg and other destinations.*

turbines too extravagant an option to consider. The now shelved gas turbine trains were designated TGS, and TGV was applied to the electric version of the train to run on the new line. Plans were changed, and electrification of the line was included. The transition of plans was made so smoothly that there was no problem in completing it on schedule.

Orders for the new trains were placed in 1976, and the first units were delivered in 1978. Each TGV is an articulated train set with power units at each end. It is electrically equipped to run on both 1500 V DC or 15,000 V AC at either 50 cycles or 16⅔ cycles (for use in Switzerland). Six 704 hp motors are mounted on the body of the power unit, two motors are mounted on each bogie of the power car, and two more are on the bogie just adjacent to the power car on the next coach, for a total of 12 motored axles.

There is no tilting mechanism on the TGV; it is not needed. The line is constructed to the needs of the train. Curves are precisely canted to allow negotiation at maximum speed at no discomfort to the passengers. There were many who criticized the French for spending $1.5 billion to construct the new line when the use of body tilting equipment might have enabled the running of high speed trains at perhaps five percent of that figure. However, the great success of the TGV and the problems that have plagued the tilting APT would seem to indicate that the French made the right decision. They certainly think so, since more special lines for TGVs are being planned.

Many who see the line for the first time comment that it has a rather strange appearance. What is strange about it is the lack of signal poles that are so familiar on most railway lines. Information on line conditions is sent over the wires

The Spanish Talgo Pendular *class 354 locomotive pulls the Madrid-Paris sleeper express.*

to computers in the cab. The engineer has a continuous series of readouts on track conditions, speed and so on right in front of him. Speed is maintained automatically once it is set by the engineer, who has plenty of other things to do in the cab of a train speeding down the track at 164 mph.

The TGV is equipped with three braking systems, all of which are operated by one controller. A dynamic braking system, based on the motors being turned into generators for braking action, can be used from top speed to about five mph. The other systems are disc and wheel tread. The usual pattern is to use the disc system lightly as the train is stopped and to apply the wheel tread brakes to clean the wheel treads.

First on-line tests began as soon as a sufficient portion of the line was ready. On 26 February 1981, a TGV set equipped with large wheels and modified gearing amongst other changes, to allow above-normal speeds was run down the track. The major purpose of the test was to see how well the track handled the speeding train. Both train and track performed admirably as the TGV reached 236 mph, a world record that still stands.

Regular commercial service over the southern parts of the line began in September 1981. It was an instant success and soon had airline executives reaching for their tranquilizers as thousands of Paris-Lyon-Marseilles business travelers a month forsook airplanes for the convenience of this train that took them from business center to business center. Speeds of 160-165 mph are commonplace on TGV runs, and increases to around 185 mph are projected for this train of tomorrow that is here today.

While electrification proceeded rapidly in France through the 1950s and 1960s, there were still nonelectrified sections that needed high-speed service. SNCF had no diesel locomotives capable of more than 87 mph, so they initiated a development project, which resulted in the RTG (*Rame à Turbine à Gaz*), a gas turbine trainset first put into regular service in 1972. The RTG is powered by an 1150 hp gas turbine, one of which is in each power car at opposite ends of the train. While the units in regular service have a maximum speed of 112 mph, an experimental version achieved speeds of 147 mph. This was a standard two-car diesel locomotive; a gas turbine was placed in the trailer car.

Ten four-car sets were ordered in 1968. These rather odd sets had a 440 hp diesel engine in one end car and a gas turbine in the other.

In 1970, these hybrids, designated ETG, were put in service on the Paris-Caen and Paris-Cherbourg routes. The Paris-Caen run was made at an average speed of 81.5 mph. The run could have been made at higher speed but laws limited top speed to 100 mph. The ETG became the RTG when the diesel was taken out and small turbines were installed in each power car.

In spite of sharply rising fuel costs, RTG trainsets have continued to operate at a profit. Two sets were sold to Amtrak in 1972.

Above: *The Soviet Type ER 200 prototype. This has achieved average speeds of 106 mph on the 400 mile Moscow-Leningrad run.*
Right: *A Netherlands 1C III EMU enters Utrecht station.*

OTHER EUROPEAN TRAINS

The ER 200 is a 14-car electric trainset built for Soviet Railways. Its intended purpose is to provide 125 mph service between Moscow and Leningrad. This is not a tilting train, since the line between Moscow and Leningrad is remarkably without curves. According to a story which may be apocryphal, Czar Alexander II was asked to designate the route. He did so, according to the story, by placing a ruler on a map and drawing a straight line beween the two cities.

The train's speed is obtained through lavish use of power. Overhead wires provide 3000 V DC to forty-eight 288 hp motors that drive axles on the intermediate cars, for a total of 13,848 hp (10,320 kW). The train has an autodriver system that automatically responds to signals which set the speed to be maintained at various points along the line.

According to Soviet Railways, the ER 200 has made the Moscow-Leningrad run (406 miles) in 3 hours and 50 minutes for an average speed of 106 mph. However, even the Soviets admit that this not the usual time. Seven hours and more is the norm.

The Netherlands Railway's ELD4 four car electric trainset provides efficient service between Amsterdam, The Hague and Rotterdam. With a maximum speed of 88 mph, the train runs on 1500 V DC supplied via catenary to eight motors suspended in the train's nose. These handsome streamlined units have been in use since 1964. They are well suited for service in a small densely-populated country such as the Netherlands which is relatively flat.

Supertrains of North America

The story of the deterioration of North American passenger service, particularly in the United States, during the 1950s, 1960s and 1970s is well known. The future looked bright for passenger service in the United States and Canada in the years immediately following World War II. The train was the way to go, and trains such as the Super Chief and the Twentieth Century Limited had assumed the status of national institutions. In 1950, a suggestion that the arch rival Pennsylvania and New York Central Railroads would be forced to merge and the merged company would go bankrupt would have been greeted with thigh-slapping laughter and a counter suggestion that you might be in need of mental help. However, even the mighty New York Central and Pennsylvania Railroads could not survive the virtual stampede of Americans away from trains and into airplanes and automobiles. By the late 1960s, railroad bankruptcies had become almost daily events. Surviving railroads petitioned the ICC (Interstate Commerce Commision) for permission to abandon passenger service.

It was clear that if passenger rail service was to survive in the United States, the Federal Government would have to intervene in some way. By this time, most railways in the world had been nationalized, but nationalization has always been anathema to Americans. Congress did respond with a series of acts in the 1960s and 1970s. One of these resulted in what many observors described as a thinly-disguised form of nationalization – Amtrak.

Amtrak, or the National Railroad Passenger Corporation, was created by an act of Congress and went into business on 1 January 1970. According to the provisions of the act, railroad companies were given permission to discontinue long-distance passenger service in return for turning over their best passenger equipment to Amtrak. Almost all American railroads jumped at the offer. Many had been unsuccessfully petitioning the ICC for permission to give up their passenger routes. The Act also provided for federal subsidies and some state and local subsidies.

As might have been predicted, Amtrak has had its share of problems, including damaging derailments, faulty equipment, and succeeding waves of administrations waving the 'We must cut the cost of government' banner, and threatening to cut off subsidies. In spite of all these problems, Amtrak has managed to replace antiquated rolling stock with some state-of-the-art equipment and to inaugurate ambitious line-improvement projects.

The National Rail Passenger Corporation Act

One of the world's great trains, Canadian Pacific's The Canadian, *crosses Stoney Creek, BC.*

was not the first government attempt to help the sagging railroads. In 1965 Congress passed the High Speed Ground Transportation Act. This Act authorized a demonstration project of high-speed self-propelled trainsets called Metroliners on the electrified route between Washington and New York, which at the time was still the Pennsylvania Railroad.

The Metroliner project had started before the Ground Transportation Act, when prototypes called MP 85s were acquired from the Budd Company in 1958. Some five years later, the City of Philadelphia helped the Pennsylvania Railroad obtained additional cars called Silverliners. The government-subsidized project called for acceleration to 150 mph in three minutes, and a top speed of 160 mph, all of which seemed rather ridiculous, since the track was in no condition for safe running of a train at that speed. All kinds of untried technology was installed in the units, and when the inevitable failures occurred, the project fell more and more behind schedule.

The Metroliner did not go into service until 1971, by which time the Pennsylvania Railroad was gone, and Amtrak logos were painted on the units. The Metroliners are not true trainsets which must run as a complete unit. Individual Metroliner cars can run alone if necessary. The cars run on 11,000 V AC picked up from overhead catenary. The current is fed to eight 300 hp motors suspended in the nose, and to one geared to each pair of wheels. The cars are fully capable of 160 mph, but they cannot run at that speed on presently existing Northeast Corridor track (164 mph was achieved on a test run). They are equipped with a dynamic braking system that operates at speeds down to 30 mph, sophisticated speed control systems, electrically-controlled doors, and telephone service.

The Metroliner was an immediate success. Although the 160 mph potential was not realized, average speeds of more than 95 mph enabled them to be competitive with New York-Washington air service, particularly since getting to a New York airport from midtown could easily take longer than the flight to Washington.

By the mid 1980s, many of the aging Metroliner units were being replaced by Amtrak's standard Amfleet rolling stock pulled by electric locomotives. Hopes for eventually achieving speeds comparable to those of the TGV and the Shinkansen were raised with the launching of the Northeast Corridor Improvement Project (NECIP) in the late 1970s. Much of the impetus for this project came from the Shinkansen trains. Millions of Americans had seen the bullet trains streaking past Mount Fuji on their television screens and

Below: *American Locomotive Company (Alco) Diesel no 4210 of the New York Central system.*
Bottom: *Union Pacific's City of Portland drawn by a M 10001 diesel.*

The Burlington Northern's Twin Cities Zephyrs.

asked the question, 'Why can't we have trains like that?' Again, as might have been expected, the NECIP fell behind schedule and consumed billions more dollars than originally projected. Despite threats of the Reagan adminstration to drastically trim or entirely eliminate funds for the project, it limped along in the 1980s. It did not seem likely that the United States would have trains with speeds rivaling those of the TGV and Shinkansen until at least the turn of the century.

While Amtrak concentrated much of its efforts in the heavily traveled Northeast Corridor, service was also continued in much of the rest of the country. However, the quality and frequency of this service has not been consistent, mainly due to frequent budget cutting by the Federal Government. The old Super Chief became the South West Limited. Amtrak retained the famous old names for many of its long-distance trains including the Chicago-Seattle Empire Builder, and the New York-Chicago Broadway Limited. However, service on these trains is spare compared to their namesakes of yore. Diners have been replaced by cafeteria-style snack bars. You stand in line to buy your clear plastic-wrapped sandwich and can of beer, which you take back to your seat to consume. In first-class, a waiter will bring this gourmet fare to your seat.

Amtrak has acquired some excellent equipment for both its electrified Northeast corridor, and diesel-hauled routes. The Amfleet coaches are comfortable and usually clean. Americans expect the air conditioning to work, and it usually does. The doors open at a touch of a bar, and passage from car to car is safe and effortless. They can be boarded at both raised platforms and at ground level. However, first-class no longer features swiveling arm chairs, an amenity sorely missed by many veteran rail riders.

As mentioned earlier, Amtrak acquired French-built RTG trainsets which were called turbo-trains in the United States, but are not to be confused with the United Aircraft turbo trains run on the Canadian National and Amtrak. The RTGs were used on a number of routes including the one followed by the Twentieth Century Limited.

Amtrak inherited many GG1s from the Penn-Central and these venerable, but dependable, machines continued to perform admirably. However, the use of such old equipment, albeit good, dependable and fast, projected a bad image. The E6CP electric locomotive was one of the first units Amtrak tried as replacements for the aging GG1s. There were also plans to change from the 25 cycle current that had always been used on the

Below: *The National Rail Passenger Corporation (otherwise AMTRAK) was formed in 1970. Despite problems caused by old rolling stock and infrastructure inherited from the railroad corporations, AMTRAK has done much to restore rail passenger service in the USA. Trials have been made with turbo power (bottom).*

Northeast Corridor to 60 cycle current supplied by commercial power companies, and the GG1s could not run on 60 cycle power.

The specifications for the new E6CP locomotive called for ability to run on both systems. The locomotive was supplied by the General Electric Company quickly by the expedient of modifying a previously existing locomotive.

Twenty-seven locomotives were delivered in 1973. Their performance has been generally satisfactory. They have a maximum speed of 85 mph, and with a horsepower rating of 7650 they could easily haul any passenger train on the New York-

Above and left: The Atchison, Topeka and Santa Fe is one of, if not the, greatest railroads in the USA. Running from Chicago to California, it is a major freight carrier, but its passenger flagship is the Super Chief, shown here. It is a fine reminder of the 1920s and 1930s when the 'Limiteds' and other fast luxury trains provided the means of long-distance continental travel.

Washington line. However, the haste to supply a dual-voltage locomotive seems nothing more than an exercise, since the current supply on the Northeast corridor has yet to be changed, although it is expected that the conversion will be completed sometime in the 1990s. The E6CPs are being replaced by the AEM-7 an electric locomotive based on a Swedish prototype.

The F40PH diesel electric locomotive has proved to be generally successful in passenger service. Built by the Electromotive Division of General Motors, this locomotive is powered by a turbocharged, 3000 hp, V-16 two-stroke diesel engine. Its maximum speed is 103 mph. The design of the F40PH was an outgrowth of derailment problems experienced with a precursor called the SDP40. The cause was traced to the design of the trucks which exerted lateral forces that caused the tracks to spread. The trucks were modified, and the frame shortened. The resulting unit became the F40PH.

Many of the F40PHs were assigned to haul Amtrak's Superliners. While these trains hardly compare to the likes of the TGV, at least in terms of speed, they did represent some of Amtrak's most ambitious efforts to provide high-quality, luxury train service. One of the superliners, the Eagle, runs from Chicago to St Louis, Dallas and San Antonio where it is joined by cars of the Sunset Limited (New Orleans-Los Angeles) for the rest of the trip to Los Angeles via Phoenix. The double-decker cars used for the Eagle provide comfortable accommodations.

Trains of the Santa Fe.
Above: *The* Super Chief *showing the raised observation windows.*
Left: *Rear view of four great trains standing at Chicago. From left to right* El Capitan, Chief, Super Chief *and another* El Capitan.
Right: *A view of the front of* El Capitan.

Top: *Via Rail Canada (VIA)'s new high speed diesel-electric LRC trains have given rail travel a new attraction. The standard on the conventional diesel trains (above) is also high. Right: Four power units, observation cars and total comfort make CP's The Canadian one of the few remaining great trains.*

Canadian Railways also suffered from competition with air and highway, but the unique organization of Canadian rails helped in the efforts to become more competitive. A private railway – the Canadian Pacific (CP) – and a national railway – Canadian National (CN) – operate in direct competition, but also in cooperation with each other. It seems to work. For one thing, Canada has true transcontinental service, something the United States never had. In 1978, in a move similar to the formation of Amtrak, an organization called Via Rail Canada took over the operation of Canadian National and Canadian Pacific passenger service.

Although Via Rail, or VIA, has experienced the usual starting difficulties and management problems, it has provided Canada with commendable passenger service. Passenger revenues have steadily increased, interesting new equipment has been obtained, and electrification is proceeding.

One of the most promising new trains run by VIA is the LRC, which stands for light, rapid, comfortable or *léger, rapide, confortable,* depending upon what part of Canada you happen to be in. The people who designed the logo went to great pains to find one whose letters would convey the same meaning in both English and French. However, wags were quick to point that the L could just as well stand for 'Lourd,' the French word for heavy. The joke had a point since the designers of the LRC insisted that one of the merits of the locomotive was its weight, which was was only 57% more than an HST (High Speed Train) car of similar capacity and performance.

The LRC is a high-speed diesel-electric locomotive designed to pull a matching train equipped with an active tilting mechanism. As such, it is similar to, but not quite the same as, the British APT. It is also similar to the APT in the problems it has experienced. Some of the conditions one can expect in Canada contributed to its problems. In winter operations, fine, powdery snow got inside the sophisticated equipment,

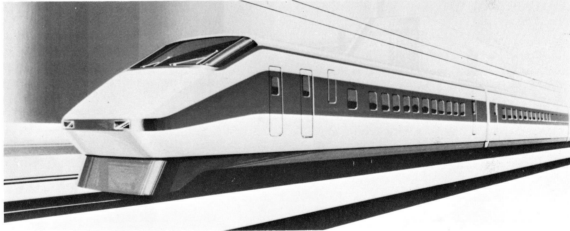

Above: *Canadian National's* Super Continental.
Right: *A Burlington Northern train carrying the slogan 'Main Street of the Northwest.'*
Left: *A proposed high speed train for California from a feasibility study done by the American High Speed Rail Corporation.*

causing all kinds of malfunctions. And, as might be expected, there have been problems with the tilting mechanism. The maximum tilt is 8½°, ½ degree less than the APT.

The locomotive is powered by a 16-cylinder 3200 hp turbocharged four-stroke diesel engine. An alternator feeds current to four DC motors suspended in the nose and geared to the axles. The locomotive itself does not tilt, a quality that enables it to be used with nontilting cars. The LRC is capable of speeds up to 125 mph. However, it has not been able to exceed 80 mph in regular service.

In spite of their difficulties, they have performed well in many of their runs. The turbo trains previously used on the CN made the Montreal-Toronto run in 4 hours and 25 minutes. The LRC is scheduled for the same 337 miles in 3 hours and 40 minutes. The turbo trains, also used for a while in the United States, were striking in appearance, but were plagued with high maintenance costs. Two LRC sets were tried by Amtrak,

and returned as not suitable for their needs.

The interiors of the cars are airy, and the seats are well designed for maximum comfort. The tilting mechanism also contributes to passenger comfort when it works.

One of the casualties of the VIA reorganization was the CN's Super-Continental, coast-to-coast service through the Rockies to Vancouver. Nevertheless, VIA can still boast of some very fine transcontinental service. The Canadian still makes seven trips each way between Montreal and Vancouver via Toronto. This is a popular train, passing through some of the most spectacular scenery in the world. Although not a high-speed train, it is not slow either. Passengers spend three nights on board making the 2896 mile journey. The sleeping accommodations are well appointed, and there are dining cars. For those who do not care to spend their money on sleeping berths or compartments, there is dayniter service. Generously proportioned seats can be steeply reclined to provide what is essentially a bed.

Supertrains of the World

The building of Japan's first railway in 1872 was one of the most significant events of the Meiji Restoration that pulled this nation out of feudalism and into the modern world. Japan's railways were constructed at 3 ft 6 in gauge rather than the 4 ft 8½ in of most other railways in the world. This variance was no handicap to Japan's railways, nor did it slow Japan's remarkable industrial development. As an island nation, Japan did not have to worry about its narrow gauge railways communicating with other lines.

Most of the country's industrial development occurred along the 350-mile Tokaido coastal strip on the southern coast of Honshu between Tokyo and Osaka. This region, which comprises less than one percent of Japan's land area, is home to 40% of Japan's population and some 75% of its industry.

The rapid industrial growth in this congested area created an urgent need for rapid transportation. However, the existing Tokaido Line between Tokyo and Osaka, built in 1889, was full of curves, gradients and countless grade crossings. There was no way to run 100 mph plus service on that line. The only thing to do was to build an entirely new line, an undertaking that was started in the late 1950s. The result was a new Tokaido line, the first of many Shinkansen lines in Japan. The word Shinkansen means simply new line.

Japan National Railways (JNR) chose to build the line at the standard gauge of 4 ft 8½ in, even though so doing would completely divorce the new line from the rest of Japan's railways. The line was electrified with 25,000 V AC rather than the 1500 V DC used on the rest of the country's electrified lines.

The construction was an awesome, formidable task. There could be no sharp curves, so instead of going around the many man-made and natural obstacles along the route, the line had to go through them. The line went through the centers of cities, necessitating buying and tearing down expensive urban properties. In spite of all these difficulties, the 320-mile line was completed in just five years.

Service was inaugurated on 1 October 1964 with the fastest trains the world had yet seen. Popularly called the bullet train because of the rounded noses of the end cars, the trainsets were capable of 160 mph. However, it was thought prudent to keep the speeds to 130 mph, still an impressive figure, and one that was more than fast enough to set a new world speed record for railways.

The Shinkansen trainsets of today are 16-car

Japanese National Railways' Shinkansen, also known as the Bullet Train, came into service in October 1964.

Above: *The Tokyo monorail.*
Left: *The Shinkansen crosses a viaduct. New lines and speeds of up to 160 mph make the bullet train network one of the most impressive in the world.*

articulated units. The current, picked up from overhead wires, is fed through step-down transformers and rectifiers to sixty-four 248 hp motors mounted on each axle. That is, every axle is motored, and each 16-car train has a peak continuously-rated horse power of 15,870. Motoring every axle enables extremely rapid acceleration. This 15,870 hp for a train with a total weight of only 834 tons is an awesome amount of power indeed.

The in-cab signalling system used on the TGV line was pioneered on the Shinkansen trains. There are no signal towers. Information on line conditions is transmitted over the wires to the cab. Changes in speed are automatically controlled. Only final approaches to a stop are under the direct control of the engineer. Japan is earthquake country. Seismographs located in the main control centers transmit signals that automatically stop all trains if an earthquake is detected.

The Shinkansen trains soon set a time of three hours and ten minutes for the Tokyo-Osaka run, for an average of 101 mph. The trains were well patronized, and by the end of the decade some 80 trains ran each way daily. There was talk of extending Shinkansen lines to a 4350-mile network, but a number of problems made that dream seem remote. The regular JNR service began to suffer catastrophic losses. The Shinkansen turned out to be a fairly noisy train, and people living or working within hearing distance were understandably disturbed. They agitated for the construction of expensive concrete sound barriers along the route. The 1973 oil crisis hit Japan very hard, causing an inflation that made the cost of new construction prohibitive.

Once again, JNR rose above its problems and

by 1975 the line had been extended into the southern island of Kyushu by the new Sanyo Shinkansen. The new route ran 664 miles from Tokyo to Hakata. The fastest service on this route makes the Tokyo-Hakata run in 6 hours and 40 minutes for an average of 110 mph. One of the outstanding civil engineering works on this line is the 11.6-mile tunnel under the Kanmon Strait, the body of water separating Honshu and Kyushu. That feat, however, is being surpassed by the 33.4-mile Seikan Tunnel under the Tsugaru Strait between Honshu and Hokkaido. At the time of this writing, it was still not certain if the railway in this tunnel would be Japan's regular 3 ft 6 in gauge or a Shinkansen.

Expansion of Shinkansen lines in a northerly direction came with the building of the Tohoku Shinkansen from Tokyo to Morioka. In contrast to the earlier projects, construction of this line consistently ran behind schedule. The Joetsu Shinkansen cuts through the Mukumi mountains, Japan's central mountain chain, from Tokyo to Niigata, a city on the north coast.

The Tohoku and Joetsu Shinkansens were constructed to handle regular service at 160 mph, but maintenance problems encountered on the original Tokaido line suggested that 130 mph had best be the maximum, at least for a while. The track and catenary take such a beating from the high speeds that the line has to be shut down periodically for maintenance. The Tokaido line had to be completely rewired and relaid after only ten years of 130 mph service. New track was laid in a bed of cast concrete slab instead of the usual sleepers set in ballast. This method helps to protect the track, but maintenance is more difficult than with the traditional road bed.

The classic photograph of the Shinkansen as it passes Mount Fuji on the Tokyo-Osaka line.

With the inauguration of 160 mph TGV service in France in 1981, the Shinkansen was no longer the fastest train in the world. The Japanese responded with trials of a prototype unit that reached 198.3 mph on a stretch of the new Tohoku line. While that was an impressive accomplishment, regular service still had to be run at a maximum of 130 mph. The French were still first, but JNR continued to work on increasing the regular running speeds of Shinkansen trains.

Although Shinkansen trains are noisy, passengers are not disturbed because of effective soundproofing. If two trains pass each other in a tunnel, automatic controls press all vestibule and entrance doors tightly against the frames, effecting an almost complete hermetic seal. Passengers' ears are protected from the abrupt changes in air pressure generated as the trains rush past each other. The interiors of Shinkansen trains are comfortable, open, and airy. Some western pasengers describe the ambience as a bit cold and crisp, not unlike a corporate reception room decorated with chrome and vinyl modern furniture.

JNR still runs fairly luxurious, reasonably fast trains on its 3 ft 6 in lines. The Kodama 8-car electric trainset is among the best known of these. These trains run at a top speed of 75 mph. Although this does not seem like much after dealing with Shinkansens and TGVs, the 50 mph average these trains set on the Tokyo–Osaka run are believed to be a record for narrow gauge railways. Earlier twelve-car versions had parlor-car first class accommodations with individual swiveling, reclining arm chairs.

CHINA

While there is nothing on Chinese railways today to compare with the TGV, HST, or Shinkansen, development and improvement is proceeding rapidly. Electrification is of top priority, and there is a strong possibility that the Chinese will be operating high speed trains before the end of the century.

Electrification and steam make sense in China, a country rich in coal and water power, but without sufficient oil. Nevertheless, building of diesel locomotives was an important component of Chairman Mao's Great Leap Forward of the 1960s. Determination to design and build their own diesel locomotives, and not be dependent on foreign technology, resulted in what amounted to a fiasco. There was plenty of zeal, but not enough experience or facilities for so heavy an industrial enterprise as building diesel locomotives.

After the Cultural Revolution faded into history, a more pragmatic approach was adopted, and they were still able to build a fleet of diesel locomotives without dependance on foreigners. Building of steam engines continued, as did use of imported diesel engines from France and Romania. One of the first successful efforts was the DF4 diesel-electric named East Wind. This is a 16-cylinder (V-16) four stroke diesel. An alternator supplies current through solid state electronics to six motors geared to the axles. It develops a total

horsepower of 3600, and can move comfortably at 70-75 miles an hour.

The Beijing followed in 1971. This is also a diesel, but rather than turning alternators or dynamos, power is transmitted to the wheels via a hydraulic torque-convertor system, similar to an automotive automatic transmission. With a top speed of 75 mph, these 3300 hp, 12-cylinder diesels have been assigned to haul the tourist trains from Beijing to the Great Wall.

Westerners find Chinese sleeping cars to be very comfortable and well maintained, as are the coaches. Dining car service and the quality of the food have also received high grades. Chinese trains are not divided into classes as such, but 'soft sleeper', although expensive, is luxurious whereas 'hard seat' tends to be extremely crowded.

AUSTRALIA

The railway situation that evolved in Australia followed the pattern of much of Australia's past history. Australia has been a unified country only since 1901, but before that time it was a collection of separate states, each of which ran its affairs as it pleased, without too much concern about

Below: The Australian XPT has achieved 144 mph in test runs. Derived from the British HST, it is due to enter service in New South Wales with improved ventilation and other modifications.

what the others did. This same attitude prevailed in the building of railways. Each state constructed its railways at whatever gauge it desired with no concern about communicating with the lines of other states. Consequently there were three different gauges in use, and there was a break of gauge

Above: An Australian National class GMI Diesel heads the Indian Pacific on the 2462-mile run from Sydney to Perth.

at practically every state border.

Building a cohesive rail system was one of the first orders of business of the new Australian Commonwealth. It was not until 1969 that a true transcontinental railway was completed in Australia. The Australians wasted no time in inaugurating luxury transcontinental train service. The first Indian Pacific pulled out in February 1970 to make the 2462-mile run from Sydney to Perth.

The Indian Pacific is not a superfast train. The trip takes some 2½ days, and the train is hauled by a rather ordinary-looking sort of diesel engine. It is quite luxurious, as indeed it should be, perhaps to distract the passengers from the fact that they are traveling though one of the most desolate, inhospitable deserts in the world.

The deluxe accommodations are two-room suites equipped with a full shower in addition to the expected amenities of toilet, basin, berths, dressing tables, lounge chairs and so on. Smaller roomettes do not have showers, but there are showers at the ends of each sleeper.

A great deal is asked of the air-conditioning on this train. Temperatures in the desert reach well into the 100s in the summer. The surface temperature on the metal sides of the cars has been known to exceed 140°F. As if in defiance of the desert, every compartment has ice water on tap in addition to the usual hot and cold. On the other hand, winters can be brutal in this area. Abrasive dust takes its toll of equipment and car surfaces in all seasons.

This route cannot be described as one that is particularly scenic unless you happen to think that treeless plains, dust and sand are scenic. However, there are those who think the desolation of central Australia has its own particular brand of beauty. The line passes through the Nullarbor Plain – the Plain of No Trees. This plain, which has been compared to the surface of the moon, is the site of the longest continuous stretch of straight track in the world – 297 miles.

The Australian State of New South Wales is investigating the possibilities of rapid inter-city service with HST units whose design is based on the British ones. The Australian version has only five cars, the engines and gearing having been modified to provide maximum regular-service speeds of 100 mph rather than 125 mph. Higher speeds would not be possible on presently-existing track, and the modified gearing improves acceleration and provides for smoother starts. Other modifications to suit the Australian environment include bogies better adapted to Australian track and a beefed-up ventilation system to cope with Australian heat and dust. An aesthetic modification is corrugated steel sides to match the Indian-Pacific coaches.

Left: *The Indian Pacific at the Perth terminal.*
Above: *'A first class hotel on wheels' is an apt description of the Indian Pacific. The trip from Sydney to Perth takes two and a half days, but the time is spent in sound-proofed air-conditioned carriages which offer a high standard of comfort and service.*

Right: *The first journey of the Indian Pacific from Perth eastward.*

Right: *Three electric locomotives haul the Blue Train up a steep gradient.*

Above and right: *Distinctive livery in blue and gold identify the Blue Train, for long the most luxurious scheduled means of rail travel. The Blue Train pulls into Fountains, Pretoria, in the mid 1970s.*

The XPT, as this train is called in Australia, achieved a speed of 144 mph in test runs, setting a new Australian record. The XPT went into regular service on three routes from Sydney and has been successful enough to encourage orders for more.

SOUTH AFRICA

South Africa's Blue Train is widely regarded as the ultimate in rail travel luxury. It has been described as a five-star hotel on wheels. Its route is between Johannesburg and Capetown, but where it is going seems unimportant. There are much faster ways to get from one of these cities to the other. South African Railways maintains that the sole purpose of the train is to provide the ultimate experience in luxury for the rail traveler.

Your name is written on the door of your Blue Train compartment, and your dining car seat is reserved just for you, again with a name card on the table. The highest level of accomodation is a three-room suite for two people. The suite includes a lounge furnished with couches and lounge chairs, a refrigerator stocked with chilled drinks, cabinets, a telephone and a radio. The beds are arranged at right angles, rather than

stacked, giving the compartment the look of a luxury liner cabin. And there is a private bath, of course. There are side tables with lamps by the beds, dressing tables, and wardrobes. The 16-car Blue Train carries only 108 people.

The Blue Train is not in competition with airlines since South African Railways owns South African Airways (SAR). SAR does a fair amount of business flying in passengers who come to South Africa just to ride the Blue Train.

Perhaps the most amazing thing about the 16-car Blue Train is that all this luxury, spaciousness and opulence is provided on a narrow gauge train – 3 ft 6 in. Much of South African rails go through mountainous country, necessitating the narrow gauge. Three electric locomotives are needed to haul the Blue Train up the steep gradients, some of which are one in fifty. Diesels are used on the stretch through the Karoo Desert between Johannesburg and Pretoria. The top speed is about 65 mph, with an average of about 35-40 mph.

The Blue Train may well be the last of a genre. Like the new Venice Simplon Orient it demonstrates that slow-paced luxury still has a place in this fast plastic-wrapped, computerized world.

What's next?

The TGV, Shinkansen, and other super trains of today have one very basic thing in common with the first trains run in the 1820s and 1830s. That is, all these trains run or ran on flanged wheels rolling on a track. The severe maintenance problems experienced on the Shinkansen, and the frustrating mechanical difficulties of the APT could well be signs that flanged wheel on rail may have reached the maximum of its potential. It seems certain that if regular railway operating speeds of 200 mph and beyond are ever to become a reality they will be attained on some kind of system other than conventional rail.

One of the earliest attempts at developing an alternative to conventional rail systems was the monorail. While monorails have been successful in some applications, they have not attained the speeds of the TGV. Also, as a rail system, it is subject to many of the same problems at high speeds as any other rail system.

A technology that has received a great deal of attention as the possible fast ground transportation of the future is hovercaft. The general idea of this kind of vehicle is movement between channeled guideways of some kind without direct contact with the base. Various power systems have been investigated. One possibility is the use of rotors somewhat like those of helicopters which would provide the power to keep the craft elevated and provide forward motion. While this principle has been successfully applied to water craft, it has not been given serious consideration for ground travel.

Magnetic levitation (maglev) is a system in which the vehicle is moved by linear electric motors, and reverse magnetic force is used for levitation. Systems are under investigation in Germany and Japan. Speeds of 500 mph and more are envisioned for systems of this kind. However, it is by no means certain if maglev will be feasible in terms of the basic technology, economics, energy consumption or environmental impact.

In the 1980s a maglev vehicle called the Transrapid-06 was being tested in Germany. The test vehicle is some 178 feet long and about 12 feet wide and runs along a T-shaped elevated guideway. Levitation is provided by 64 electromagnets, and the guiding system consists of 56 electromagnets. Energy to move the train is provided via a stator which is placed along the top surface of the guideway. In essence, the train itself is an electric motor. That is, it is the rotor, the part of an electric motor that moves when energy is supplied through the stator.

The configuration of the base of the train is such that it wraps around the guideway in a kind

Kraus-Maffei of Munich, Germany, designed this futuristic maglev unit.

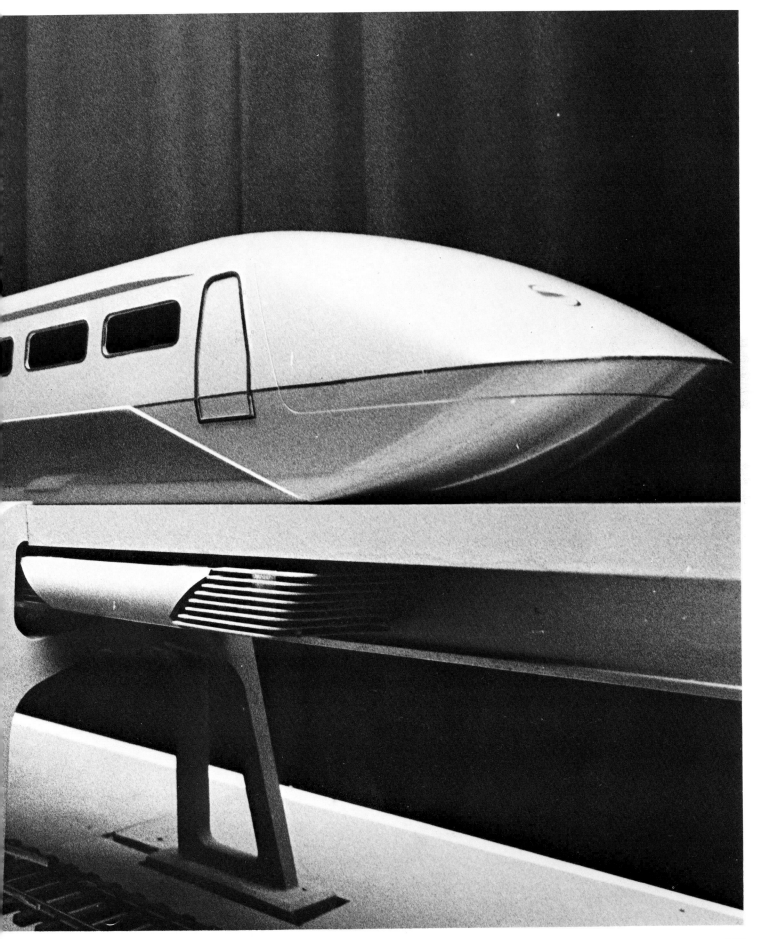

Right: *The German Transrapid 06 maglev train in mock-up form.*
Above: *The Transrapid 06 maglev train undergoes tests at the Emsland Test Facility. It is powered by a linear motor propulsion unit and is designed to carry 200 passengers at up to 250 mph.*

of C shape. The guidance magnets are in the crook of the C and lie opposite the outer edge of the guideway. The levitation magnets are on the inner surface of the ends of the C, placed so they are under the guideway. The levitation magnets exert a longitudinal magnetic flux, lifting the vehicle, while the guidance magnets exert a magnetic flux perpendicular to the track.

The two-car Transrapid-06 has moved at speeds in excess of 200 mph on 20-mile test guideway between Doerpen and Lathen in northern Germany. One advantage it seems to have over high speed flange on track is that it is much quieter than trains such as the Shinkansen. Research continued through the mid-1980s, although the West German government cut development funding.

The German maglev has no wheels, while the Japanese system is equipped with retracting wheels for use at low speeds. Maglev trains can be thought as actual low-flying vehicles. In that sense, the wheels of the Japanese version could be thought of as landing gear. The German system has no wheels, and in general is regarded as simpler than the Japanese version. However, the Japanese system is faster, having moved at 320 mph.

If the Transrapid succeeds, it could well be adopted in the United States. The United States

The Hitachi monorail which provides a local service for Kita-Kyushu City, Japan.

Above: *Japanese National Railways' experimental high-speed maglev vehicle on a test track.*
Right: *The Wuppertal suspended monorail in action.*

Department of Transportation has approved a study of Transrapid for a possible high-speed link between Los Angeles and Las Vegas.

The private sector is also involved in planning high-speed railways in the United States. In the 1980s, a company called American High-Speed Rail was well along in planning a TGV-type electric high speed train to run between Los Angeles and San Diego. The company nurtured hopes of having a system in operation by the early 1990s. At the time of writing, it was not certain if the train itself would be American-made of imported from France or Japan. Using American-made technology has advantages in terms of providing jobs and appeal to patriotic sentiment. However, the use of proven technology would no doubt result in an operating system becoming a reality much more quickly than would be the case with designing a new vehicle.

High-speed rail systems just might have a chance in the United States. The airways are becoming crowded, presenting serious questions of safety. The time required to get to big-city airports often negates the time gained from flying.

Ironically, high-speed rail might be the answer to that problem. Although there was an apparent oil glut in the 1980s, it is inevitable that the supply will dwindle, forcing prices up, and once again making rail travel the way to go.

INDEX

ACKNOWLEDGMENTS

Alco Historic Photos: 84 (top); G. Freeman Allen:
28-9, 30, 41 (bottom), 42-3, 49 (bottom), 60-61, 64,
65 (bottom), 68 (top and bottom), 72, 76, 78-9
(both), 80-81 (both), 101 (top), 102, 104 (top), 108-
9 (both), 109 (top), 110, 110-111; G. Freeman Allen/
MARS: 14 (top); American High Speed Rail
Corporation: 93 (bottom); Amtrak: 86 (both);
Australian Tourist Commission: 102-3; BBC Hulton
Picture Library: 12 (top), 32-3, 34, 36 (bottom), 39
(both), 44, 71 (top inset); British Rail: 73 (bottom),
74-5 (bottom); British Rail/MARS: 73 (top);
Burlington North Railroad: 2-3, 6-7, 85, 92;
Canadian National Railways: 93 (top); Canadian
Pacific Corporate Archives: 82-3, 91; Compagnie
Internationale des Wagon-Lits et du Tourisme: 8-9,
24, 45, 46-7 (top), 47 (bottom), 49 (top), 50 (all); DB
Mainz/MARS: 68 (middle); DeGolyer Library,
Southern Methodist University: 21 (top); Mikio
Ebihara: 4-5; German Information Center: 35, 69
(both), 106-7, 108 (top); Illustrated London News
Picture Library: 48; Italian State Railways/MARS: 65
(top), 66; Japan Information Center: 98-99; Japan
National Tourist Organization: 96; Japanese National
Railways: 97; Koyusha, Japan/MARS: 94-5; Library of
Congress Collection: 18-19; Mansell Collection: 25;
New South Wales State Railways/MARS: 100-101;
New York Public Library Picture Collection: 13, 14
(bottom), 15 (top), 17; PHMC Railroad Museum of
Pennsylvania: 20-21; Pullman Company/MARS: 21
(bottom); Rail Archive Stephenson/Hepburne-Scott:
38; Santa Fe Industries Inc: 86-7, 87, 88-9 (all);
Science Museum, London: 12 (bottom), 30-31, 31
(top); SNCF, Paris/MARS: 1, 40, 62, 75 (top); South
African Railways/MARS: 104 (bottom), 105; Brian
Stephenson: 10-11, 12, 14-15, 42-3, 56, 63, 66-7, 67
(top), 70-71, 71 (bottom), 74 (top), 77; Swiss
National Tourist Office: 58-9; Union Pacific Railroad
Museum Collection: 36-7 (top), 37, 84 (bottom);
Venice Simplon Orient-Express: 52-3, 54 (both), 55
(all), 57 (both); Via Rail, Canada: 90 (bottom); La
Vie du Rail/MARS: 41 (top); La Vie du Rail/J N
Westwood: 26, 27; West Australian Government
Railways, Perth/MARS, London: 103 (bottom); J N
Westwood: 22-23.